≪ Praise for YOU ARE A BRAND! ≫

"You Are a Brand! *is the primer for anyone who wants to do more with their career, their life, or their business.*"
— **Lynn Zimmerman, President, Sales Mindshare;**
coauthor, *Learn the Secrets*

"You Are a Brand! *contains valuable information and exercises. Kaputa's approach completely turned my career around.*"
— **Kat Connelly, President, Kat Connelly Productions**

"*Whether you want to change the world or simply change how you are perceived, you'll find everything you need to know about developing a powerful visual identity and verbal identity and then some. I know from personal experience that Kaputa's insights about how to tap into branding power work.*"
— **Laura Berkowitz Gilbert, Principal, Boomerang Studio**

"*Reading* You Are a Brand! *is like getting the inside scoop to building your own successful business or career.*"
— **Susan Sommers, fashion and business comportment coach**

→You Are A BRAND!

How Smart People **Brand** Themselves
>> for **Business Success**

CATHERINE KAPUTA

NICHOLAS BREALEY
PUBLISHING

BOSTON • LONDON

Paperback edition first published by Nicholas Brealey Publishing in 2010.

20 Park Plaza, Suite 1115A   3-5 Spafield Street, Clerkenwell
Boston, MA 02116, USA   London, EC1R 4QB, UK
Tel: + 617-523-3801   Tel: +44-(0)-207-239-0360
Fax: + 617-523-3708   Fax: +44-(0)-207-239-0370
                        www.nicholasbrealey.com

Special discounts on bulk quantities of Nicholas Brealey books are available to corporations, professional associations, and other organizations. For details, contact us at 888-273-2539.

Printed in the United States of America.
14 13 12 11 10   8 7 6 5 4 3 2 1

ISBN: 978-1-85788-545-3

Previously published as *U R a Brand!* by Davies-Black in 2005.

The Library of Congress has previously catalogued this edition as follows:
Kaputa, Catherine
U R a brand : how smart people brand themselves for business success /
Catherine Kaputa.—1st ed.
p. cm.
Includes index.
ISBN 978-0-89106-213-4
1. Professions—Marketing. 2. Career development. 3. Success in business.
I. Title.
HD8038.A1K36 2006
650.1—dc22
2005025361

For my beloveds,
Mike
and
Ramsey

Thence comes it that my name receives a brand.

William Shakespeare
Sonnet 111

CONTENTS

‹‹ Foreword ››

There are only two things in life worth striving for. One is happiness; the other is success.

There are a lot of happy people who aren't very successful. And there are a lot of successful people who aren't very happy. But if you have both, what more could you want?

Money? Not really. Money can't buy happiness. And most truly successful people have more money than they will ever spend.

Happiness and success, the yin and the yang of life. Like the Chinese symbols for all the principles one finds in the universe, the yin and the yang are diametrically opposed concepts. Which is why it is very difficult to achieve both at the same time.

To be happy, you need to create a positive attitude in your own mind. A powerful sense of self, so to speak. Or, as a cynic might say, "A legend in one's own mind." Let's call this the "yin."

To be successful, you need to create positive attitudes in the minds of other people. You can't make yourself successful. Only other people can make you successful.

In the same way, you can't make a sale. Only other people can decide whether to buy from you, be you an individual or a company.

In other words, you need to build a "self-brand," a reason for people to buy from you, whether you are selling yourself for a job or selling products and services to others. Let's call this the "yang."

Most people focus on the yin. It's logical. If you can create a powerful positive attitude about yourself, this attitude will rub off on other people. They will perceive you to be the successful person you are trying to become.

That's why you can find thousands of books on this subject—*The Power of Positive Thinking* by Norman Vincent Peale, for example.

The yin is conventional wisdom wrapped in a positive thinking package: Hard work, total dedication, constant improvement in every aspect of your life are bound to bring you not only happiness but also the success you believe you deserve.

Conventional wisdom is always wrong. Positive thinking might make you happy (the yin), and it is a terrific approach to life in general, but it won't bring you success. To become successful, you need to focus on the yang.

You need to focus on creating a positive attitude in the minds of other people. In other words, you need to create a self-brand.

Building a product brand and building a self-brand require similar strategies. The problem is that building a self-brand goes against a person's natural instincts. Take one example: Most people think of themselves as "well rounded," with an interest in all aspects of life: art, music, theater, sports, politics, etc. A great way to live a happy life, a lousy way to build a brand.

But that's getting into the heart of Catherine Kaputa's message.

I first met Catherine when she worked with us at our New York City advertising agency, Trout & Ries. That was over 20 years ago, but I have always remembered her and her participation in the many meetings that took place in the ad agency.

She was always the smartest person in the room.

Now it's nice to be smart, but that doesn't necessarily make you successful, as Catherine points out in this book. Sometimes being smart is a handicap. Smart people are often too smart to take advice from others.

I hope that's not true about you. (And it probably isn't if you've picked up this book.)

What is also remarkable about Catherine is that she has taken her own advice. She has built her self-brand by following the same principles you can read about in this book.

You should do the same. But you have to forget about the yin and focus on the yang. You have to focus on those strategies that will build your self-brand in the minds of others, even though many of those strategies go against conventional wisdom.

Happiness and success, the yin and the yang of life. Assuming you have the yin under control, let Catherine Kaputa lead you through the steps you need to take to achieve the yang.

A success that might go well beyond anything you could possibly imagine.

—Al Ries
coauthor, *The Origin of Brands*

‹‹ Preface ››

Some things have changed since the hardcover version of this book came out in 2006. Some things never change.

The branding ideas in this book are timeless: they work in expanding markets, they work in contracting markets. However, economic uncertainty can be a catalyst to add urgency to working on your personal brand and finally taking control of your future.

The last few years have been a wonderful adventure and I've enjoyed meeting new people while giving "You are a Brand!" presentations and workshops at corporations and organizations across the country. My concern for the difficult and changing role of women in the workplace inspired me to write a second book, *The Female Brand*. I'm thrilled that *You Are a Brand*! has been an inspiration to so many people and now with the paperback edition, I hope that many more people can benefit from its message.

In the personal-branding mindset, you are your most important asset—an asset, like education, that no one can take away from you. Personal branding shows you how to maximize the value of that asset, both in terms of self-actualization—becoming who you can be—and in terms of human capital—maximizing the financial value of your career. Yet personal branding is not taught in school and has become the most neglected aspect of education.

Here's an example of the difference personal branding can make. As a mid-level executive at a large company—a client I'll call "Marisa"—had ambition, worked hard, and did a great job. Marisa sometimes found herself in the elevator with the CEO of her division. Before developing a personal branding mindset, Marisa spent this valuable opportunity making small talk with the CEO about the weather.

After learning to focus on her brand image, Marisa realized her "elevator speech" was branding her as the weather girl! Vowing not to blow off these opportunities any more, she started sharing business anecdotes about her team and its accomplishments. She soon became branded as a high potential employee on the fast track.

Thinking like a brand means creating a brand for yourself and marketing it, and not squandering the opportunities that constantly come your way. It's easy to shortchange yourself if you're not thinking like a brand.

The good news is, anyone can join the personal branding club. And this book can make you a member. Welcome to the club!

⟨⟨ Introduction ⟩⟩

Success as a corporate executive in a Fortune 500 company (or as an employee in any type of company these days) requires careful, calculated branding, both to enter onto the playing field and to stay in the game.

Success also requires a dose of that great universal mystery we call "luck," that inexplicable combination of things, time, and actions and their infinite juxtapositions. But luck is not something you can count on, although there are practical things you can do to manifest more of it in your life, which this book explains.

You Are a Brand! is a field guide to success in business or whatever realm you are exploring.

You'll get the inside scoop—the secrets and hidden rules of success of people on the move from all walks of life—from a self-brand strategist who helped them on their journey. You'll learn how the branding principles and strategies developed for the commercial world may be used to achieve your business and personal potential.

In short, you are a brand.

Top entertainers, politicians, and athletes have long used branding principles and strategy to create stardom. Now, savvy professionals, businesspeople, and entrepreneurs are also using self-, or personal, branding, so that they can be more successful.

If you study the lives of successful entrepreneurs, well-known business executives, politicians, performers, and the like, you'll discover that hard work or luck alone wasn't instrumental in their achievement. Rather, their success was the result of a conscious process, a strategic branding process, often undertaken with the assistance of advisers, coaches, and other mentors who propelled their achievements and celebrity.

How to achieve success is a key theme in this book: professional success in terms of getting paid what you're worth, landing the promotion you deserve, or launching a start-up that lasts. But self-branding doesn't benefit just you, and it's a mistake to think of it only in terms of self-promotion. Self-branding is a strategic process that benefits the company you work for or are building. It shows you how to bring more value to your company, your clients, and your projects by being focused and strategic, by having top-notch communication, sales, and marketing skills, and by having a valuable network of business and personal contacts. I am also going to talk about success in a larger sense, in terms of self-actualization—being who you were meant to be. Branding is a great tool for both, because it makes you an active partner in your business and in your life destiny.

You Are a Brand! will teach you self-branding strategies and career moves you won't learn in business school or anywhere else.

You'll discover the career and perception problems faced by senior-level executives like Benjamin, who had to unite competing department heads around a compelling vision when he took over as president of a technology company. You'll meet sophisticated up-and-comers like Anthony, who had a fairy-tale life and a Wall Street salary until his world came crashing down on 9/11. You'll meet new entrepreneurs like Lynn, a sales professional who built a reputation for herself and her sales insights that led to a business start-up. You'll meet people like Kate, whose boss didn't think she deserved the title and salary of her peers even though she was handling the same workload.

You Are a Brand! is for people of all stripes who must be brand builders if they are to succeed in today's dynamic and challenging marketplace. This book is for ambitious people who want to do more with their lives. It is for people who want to consciously create success and perhaps also achieve high visibility and renown.

It is for people who want to reposition and rebrand themselves for a second act. It is for entrepreneurs, professionals, and business owners who want to fuse their personal and company brands into identities that will help them achieve maximum impact. It is for kids and teenagers, and even their parents, who want the best school brand stamped on their résumés because it will give them a head start.

It is especially for women, women like myself, who were told as children, "Don't upstage your brother" or "It's not nice to call attention to yourself." The truth is, if you don't brand yourself, someone else will, and it probably won't be the brand you had in mind.

You Are a Brand! will make the principles of branding available to you. In many ways, brands are like people: They have qualities, attributes, and personalities. And people are like brands. They are products that can be nurtured and cultivated to become winning brands.

You'll learn how to package your brand with a powerful visual and verbal identity without seeming promotional or obnoxious. You'll be introduced to 10 strategies from the commercial world and shown how they can be applied to you. Each chapter contains examples, tips, and brainstormer exercises so that you can implement the branding process in your life. You will learn how to maximize the potential of your most important asset—you.

In short, this book will give you control over how you are perceived.

If anyone understands this, I do. I spent two decades as a branding and advertising expert.

A dominant theme or clichéd example of the classic branding story would be that of the young, ambitious executive on the way up; the clichéd location would be New York City; the clichéd company would be on Madison Avenue or Wall Street; and the clichéd person would be me. I'm Catherine Kaputa, and I lived that cliché.

I grew up in the 1950s and 1960s as did 77 million other Americans. If I were any more typical, I'd start to become untypical; so I think most readers can relate because they either are part of the baby-boom brand or have been unduly influenced or annoyed as this dominant brand made its way through the last half of the 20th century and into the first half of the 21st century.

Dad was a genuine war hero, like many others of his generation. He piloted 35 missions over Germany during World War II and had numerous medals that branded him as a war hero. He also had the ultimate hero branding 50 years later: interment with honors at Arlington National Cemetery. Dad was sent to Miami once for R&R. He loved it and vowed to return there to live if the Nazis didn't get him first. Dad was packaged in the strong silent personality that was a powerful draw for men of his generation, the group Tom Brokaw branded as "the greatest generation."

Miami and the world seemed so innocent then. We rode our bikes to school and everywhere else without supervision, played marbles and hopscotch at recess, and saw the future in terms of unrelenting rapid progress. Frank Sinatra sang the theme song, and it came from Miami Beach, too: "He's got high hopes. He's got high apple pie in the sky hopes."

Who could resist the brand of an era? I had "apple pie in the sky hopes," too, particularly in my adolescence.

Everybody's been there. Adolescence: It's personal identity time, it's absurd, it's profound, it's scary. The culture was still offering limited roles for women, and I admit I didn't have the courage or creativity to face the future without a role model. The one that intrigued me was Brenda Starr, reporter, the heroine of a comic strip. She was glamorous, powerful, and respected and got to travel all over. Journalism. That was the brand for me.

So off I went to Northwestern University and the Medill School of Journalism. Then, caught up in the identity crisis of my generation in the late '60 and early '70s, I switched gears. For the next eight years, Japanese art became my life and brand.

I was in deep: master's degree from the University of Washington, Seattle Art Museum curator job, Asian art books published, Smithsonian Fellow, Tokyo University study grant. I applied for the Ph.D. program at Harvard because Harvard was right for my brand (high hopes again). Just as I was organizing my dissertation for my Ph.D., my general uneasiness morphed into an epiphany. This is not me. This is not my brand. I want out! Dr. Kaputa was not going to happen. I took two aspirins and cried all morning.

You don't need a connection to New York City to feel its influence, but I did have a connection, and that made the city's gravity a force I could not resist. Heart and head were both pulling me. I still wasn't sure what I was going to do, but I knew where I would do it. The capital of the world.

It's been said, "You can't start off in New York; you need to play Peoria first." No you don't. I didn't.

I sold my Volkswagen Beetle, crashed at Aunt Sophie's in the Bronx, and was determined to find an exciting job in my first love—communications. The vagueness of the communications brand was the proper mind-set, since it gave me the flexibility to brand myself to an opportunity (journalism, advertising, public relations), and I needed flexibility. My previous brand was a handicap.

"Why does an Asian art scholar want to be in advertising?" was the refrain. But persistence does pay off. One ad agency interpreted my background as "creative," and I had a foot in the door.

The mark of a hot ad shop was big-name national accounts and talked-about TV campaigns. Trout & Ries didn't have sexy creative; rather, it was a hotbed of brand strategy and positioning. I was pretty mediocre in my first job as a copywriter. I found that my strengths were more on the account side than on the creative side. "Creative" had been the right brand to land the job, but my gut was pushing me to reposition my brand.

Al Ries and Jack Trout, by the way, rebranded themselves after I left. Each changed his brand position from "ad agency chief" to "marketing strategist," found the right brand position, and took off. (Boy, how brand image can change. Today, when I tell people my background, the "Wow!" is always about my having worked in my first job under the now-famous branding gurus Al Ries and Jack Trout.)

My personal career strategy was to move on to a larger, well-known agency so I could gain experience on a high-profile brand.

I was already branded as a "small agency" person after my four years at Trout & Ries. The recruiters were of one stripe: "You don't have 'big agency' experience."

When others can't help, do it yourself! In this case, I networked, talked to people, found old friends, made new friends. It worked, plus I got lucky. (Strange phenomenon: The harder you work, the more luck you have.) I landed a job at Wells Rich Greene managing the "I ❤ NY" account.

Mary Wells Lawrence had already achieved legendary status by the time I arrived at the agency in 1982. She was a woman of style and was as clever with her personal brand as she was with her extremely successful campaigns, which include Braniff's colorful planes, Alka-Seltzer's "Plop plop fizz fizz," and Benson & Hedges 100s. Mary was a Francophile, and the place was run like the French court, so it was always an interesting place to work.

The "I ❤ NY" account was a wonderful piece of business to work on. The TV commercials featuring Broadway musicals and celebrities received numerous creative awards and became a flagship creative account for the agency. Part of my job was to work with the Broadway Theater League to secure the Broadway talent and enlist other celebrity talent to appear in the commercials.

Celebrities don't exist without branding, and they're good at it, but their public brands are not always real. I won't be telling you who made outrageous demands, but I'll tell you about one of the most impressive stars who came in to pitch New York.

Mr. High Hopes himself, Ol' Blue Eyes, lived up to his brand. I was struck by his mesmerizing, alert, bright blue eyes. They really were special, as were his purposefulness and demeanor. He was shorter than I had imagined, but bigger than I had expected, too. He paid his own way on this pro bono gig when others wanted freebies for themselves and their entourages.

Frank Sinatra was a famous brand and had done some well-known rebranding in his time, from teen idol crooner to movie star to singer for the ages. Along the way, he also went through some negative branding as a Mafia associate and brawler. But we were very dear friends for about twenty minutes on the "I ❤ NY" commercial shoot, and my impression of his brand can be described in one word: class.

My next career strategy was to become a corporate advertising director. Ad agencies are notorious for wanting young people and discarding old people, and I was in my thirties. Their unspoken rationale is that they need fresh ideas and young bodies willing to work long hours, and the perception is that those things are the province of the young. So my goal became to grow old at a big company, with a big title and a big office and big money.

The recruiters were no help. They see only your past, not your future. They pegged me as an agency person, not a corporate advertising director. So I was on my own, networking. The lesson in networking is to pursue all leads no matter how obscure—even a friend of a friend of a friend of a friend, and don't stop there. Salespeople will tell you it's a numbers game, and they're right.

Through a remote contact, I got a Wall Street interview, and voilà! I landed my dream job, director of advertising at Shearson Lehman Brothers. I would end up staying for fifteen years. My title stayed more or less the same, but the firm's name changed again and again, and it was Smith Barney when I left.

You can imagine the branding challenges that came with all the identity changes and the complex nature of Wall Street businesses. Corporate branding and advertising are not just about naming products and making commercials. You need smart positioning, communications strategy, and marketing tactics. And I was pretty good at it. Maybe someday I'll write a book on the subject.

Many influences affect our brands. Many can be analyzed and explained. Many cannot. Cause and effect are certain only in pure science. Branding is a science in the way social science is a science, with the "science" part of the term based on the fantasy that human behavior can be quantified. In reality, branding's cause-and-effect relationship is never certain. Be grateful for all your experiences. It's your input that makes them help or hurt.

What's important to know is that anything can happen and even bad things can have good results. I learned through fortune and misfortune to take control of my branding and to try to understand branding influences in the larger world.

Did I make mistakes? Of course, lots of them. The only people who haven't made mistakes are people who never did anything, and that's a mistake, too.

Was I successful? Well, I did what I wanted to do, and I didn't get hurt, wasn't miserable, and didn't become poverty-stricken in the process. Having desires or goals and then working to accomplish them is as close as we get to the idea of success, and it's available to everybody, even with our flaws and limitations.

Thanks, Universe; thanks, Planet; thanks, America; thanks, New York; thanks, Miami; thanks, Mom; thanks, Dad.

Author's note: In recounting the self-branding odysseys of many clients, I used pseudonyms to disguise the identity of the individuals involved. Details such as industry, location, and other distinguishing factors were often modified or camouflaged in order to protect the privacy of individuals and companies.

None of these changes affect the basic substance of a story. The purpose was to disguise identity yet provide the key experiences, strategies, and action plans that would be of benefit to others.

‹‹ Acknowledgments ››

I couldn't have written this book without people. After all, self-branding is about people.

This book started with an idea, an idea that wouldn't die in spite of the thick file of rejection letters from literary agents and publishers. Then, Connie Kallback, the acquisitions editor at Davies-Black Publishing, found me through a networking contact. Connie supported my book through round one, when her publishing team asked me to refocus my proposal and resubmit it. I thought it was a polite way of turning me down, so I looked into self-publishing. But Connie, true to her name, called back. And here we are, ready to hit the presses. Thank you, Connie. You are the best editor an author could hope for. And thanks to the rest of the Davies-Black team: Laura Simonds, Laura Ackerman-Shaw, Jill Anderson-Wilson, and Francie Curtiss.

I must name Al Ries in this list. Al gave me my start in the world of advertising and branding. And it took some faith, since I had spent the previous eight years doing graduate work in Japanese art history. No other ad agency would let me in the door with those credentials. (Of course, it helped that an employee quit two days after my interview, so my timing was lucky.) During my four years working at his agency, Al taught me the ropes about brand strategy and advertising. His way of thinking and writing has always been an inspiration, so I am thrilled that he said yes when I asked him to write the foreword to my book. Thanks, Al.

I owe a large debt to my clients, who let me get involved in their stories, ideas, and makeovers. Clients who let me work with them to find the magic that was in them and in the world around them all along.

Three clients, Lynn Zimmerman, Kat Connelly, and Laura Berkowitz Gilbert, went above and beyond the call of duty for this project. Lynn was always a sounding board and a personal cheerleader. Kat read many of the chapters and offered smart suggestions. Laura designed the book cover and interior, and gave the graphics some real brand attitude. I owe many thanks to clients and business associates, and especially to Sandy Evans, Jeff Mamera, George Pine, Susan Somers, Mike James, and

Ralph Guild. There is a large group of clients whom I must thank anonymously. I used pseudonyms in the book to protect their privacy, but they allowed me to share their stories so that readers might benefit. Thank you all.

I am grateful to family members who were willing to indulge me in this project as I searched for a writing voice and a publisher. Thanks to my cousin Gary Gulkis, who provided editorial inspiration for three of the early chapters, and long ago introduced me to the powerful words of the Bard. Thanks to my sisters, Kevin Bishop, Jean Anderson, and Joan Ford, who heard me talk about this project on the phone more times than they would like to remember. Thanks also to my cousin Roberta Maguire, who happily read the entire manuscript.

And then there are the friends and business colleagues who were a wonderful support network, especially Virginia Portillo, Vasso Petrou, and Diane Morgan. Thanks to my friend Margaret Yelland, who read a very early, badly written draft and still encouraged me to persist. And thanks to my North Miami High School chum Nancy Capizzi DeMeo, who introduced me to Stan Wakefield, the book agent who got my book published. There are other friends, business colleagues, and acquaintances too numerous to mention who shared insights, offered support, or read a chapter. Thank you all.

Finally, there is Mike and our son, Ramsey. Mike is no doubt thinking, "It's about time this is finished!" And Ramsey will be happy to have his mom pay more attention to him than to her laptop. Mike has been my biggest supporter as this project took over my, and our, life. His belief in me and support of my desire to put these ideas and stories into a book never wavered. Mike, I couldn't have done it without you. Thanks.

TAKE CHARGE OF
YOUR SELF-BRAND

> *Our remedies oft in ourselves do lie.*
>
> **William Shakespeare**
> *All's Well That Ends Well* **(I, 1)**

Branding is about *soft power*. For companies today, it's not the *hard things*—tangibles like bricks and mortar, equipment and inventories—that contribute the most to a company's value. It's *soft things*—the brands and company reputation, the ideas and intellectual capital, the consumer relationships and business alliances—that have the most value.

Like it or not, branding and soft power affect us every day because they influence how we feel about something. Few of us make the decision to buy something after carefully testing and considering the merits of the different brands on the market. No one goes out and does a blind taste test of colas and then selects the one that *objectively* tastes best. Even if it's a more expensive (and consequently more considered) purchase, like a car or a laptop, we will compare hard things like product features and performance criteria, but we will decide based on soft things such as what the brand represents to us.

It's the same with people. It isn't the hard, quantifiable things, like educational credentials, experience, and job titles, that contribute the success. The real power lies in harnessing soft power—strategy and tactics, image and visual identity, words and verbal identity, visibility and reputation, and other branding ideas—all the things that will help attract people to you.

Business success, like brand success, depends on what other people think about you. If people think you are a dynamic business leader, you are. If people think you're a B player, you are (until you change their perceptions). It doesn't matter what is "objectively" true. Perception is reality.

Creating positive impressions in the minds of other people is the work of self-branding. It used to be about "Can you do the job?" Now, many people can do what you do. So it has to be about something more. Above all, branding is a strategic process. The goal is to provide that something more to succeed in a changing, highly competitive business environment (and to be authentic and even to enjoy yourself in the process).

This book is about how you can tap into soft power—your self-branding power—and harness it for career and life success.

FIND YOUR "BIG IDEA"

You are your most important asset. In a sense, you are your only asset. And your ability to maximize the asset that is *you* is the single most important ingredient in your success.

That's why self-branding is so valuable. For people, branding is about achieving greater success, as represented by money, fame, self-esteem, or whatever measure is important to you.

But I am also talking about becoming who you were meant to be, which means that success includes becoming who you truly are. The trick to effective self-branding is to devise a strategy that works in achieving professional and life goals but also is true to you—that brings more of you into the equation.

Branding for people is about finding your Big Idea—your unique selling proposition (USP). You want to represent something special—a belief system you stand for that sets you apart from others. This could be made up of your point of view, your vision, your style, even your mystique—the X Factor that makes you special and relevant.

Branding for people is also about "packaging" the brand that is you and using branding strategies and principles from the commercial world

---

SELF-BRAND: A **person** represents a skill set. A **self-brand** represents a Big Idea, a belief system, that other people find special and relevant.

---

to enhance your identity and communicate your USP. It also means developing a personal marketing plan for reaching your goals, tactics to get from A to B (and through all the other letters of the alphabet, depending on your goals). And it means engaging your target audience without seeming self-promotional and obnoxious. This book will show you how.

LEVERAGE BRAND POWER

Looking at yourself as a brand has enormous advantages. The truth is that being good, by itself, doesn't guarantee success. We all know talented people who are underemployed, underpaid, or even unemployed.

With branding, you learn how to look at yourself as a product in a competitive framework. Branding is the process of differentiating that product—you—from the competition and taking action steps to get where you want to go.

Branding also requires that you target a market. A market is any group of people that you need to engage with in order to reach your goals. Clients or customers are a target market, as are the prospects you are pursuing. If you work at a company, you should view your colleagues and direct reports as target markets. Don't overlook your boss. In any company, your boss is probably your most important target market. Recruiters, industry leaders, and even competitors are also markets for your self-brand.

Branding shows you how to attract a market. Don't think in terms of what you want to say and do. Flip it. Think in terms of the reaction you want from your target market. And what you have to do to get that reaction.

Branding also gives you a template for developing a marketing program directed at your key target markets. You will learn how to develop ic brand messages and tactics for maximizing success with your target market as well as methods of measuring your success.

Self-branding is not just good for you personally, it is good for the company, too. Branding teaches you how to be more strategic by staying relevant to the market and the latest thinking. It teaches you how to use advertising techniques to build a powerful verbal identity to express your ideas through signature words and expressions. Branding teaches you how to package your ideas for a strong visual identity, too, so they will break through and be remembered. And it teaches you how to use other branding techniques to build consensus and lead in today's competitive global marketplace.

Any way you slice it, brands win over products hands down. A branded item is viewed as better than its generic counterpart. Brands are perceived as higher in quality. They are in demand. They sell for a premium price.

Generic products compete only on price, by offering a very low price. (And if you're reading this book, I doubt that you want to compete that way.) As shown below, the list of a brand's advantages goes on and on.

BRAND	VS.	PRODUCT
Is bought		Has to be sold
Creates emotional bond		Creates no attachment
Has high visibility		Has low visibility
Is unique		Is a commodity
Endures		Becomes outdated
Has premium price		Has low price
Creates buzz		Is of low interest
Stays relevant		Is static
Is memorable		Is forgettable

TAKE CHARGE OF YOUR BRAND

My mantra to my clients is "You are a brand!" This book will take you through stories, examples, and brainstormer exercises to help you make yourself a brand.

The first thing you need to do is to commit. You must take an active rather than a passive role in defining yourself and your future.

Developing a winning self-brand requires some work. The left-brain work involves analyzing facts and trends as well as planning tactics. Right-brain work involves tapping into your intuition and creativity as you develop a personal-brand strategy, a visual identity (your packaging), and a verbal identity (your self-brand messages) in order to reach your goals.

Before you can develop a successful self-brand, you need to decide what you want. You need to ask and answer questions about who you are, where you are now, and what you want to do with your life and career.

Of course, for many of us, this is the sticky part. These are the very issues we tend to avoid until we're in a crisis. Or we live a life in which there is conflict between who we are, what we want, and where we are heading.

I often recognize this disconnect in statements like "I'm doing X now because I fell into it, but I really want to be doing Y in the future" or "I'm in it for the money, but I need something more rewarding in the future." One client told me, "I went into law because my father is a country lawyer, an icon really, like Atticus Finch in *To Kill a Mockingbird*, but I hate it. To me, law is drudgery. I long for more creative lifework."

Even though people want success, some resist self-branding because they feel that it's unseemly to think strategically and creatively about themselves and then present themselves in the best possible light. It's too calculated.

I recently met with someone who had this problem. Hal was a talented lawyer in general practice, but his business was struggling. He was referred to me by a friend who hadn't gone to the elite law school Hal had attended yet was getting top dollar for his legal counsel. Hal's friend had carved out a high-profile niche for himself as a white-collar criminal defense attorney.

When I talked to Hal about narrowing the focus of his business and developing a name for himself in that specific area, he balked. "I don't want to resort to selling myself. I have a law degree from a top school, and I won't stoop to becoming a salesperson."

Which would you rather be—a top lawyer or a top-credentialed lawyer?

LIVE YOUR DREAM

Our work fantasies often reflect desires that we have put on hold in our lives. Many people light up when I ask them to describe their dream jobs. "Oh, if I could live my dream, here's what I'd be doing." And they go on to recount something that has always intrigued them and been at the back of their minds, but which they have never pursued or acted on.

But as workplace philosophers such as William Bridges and John Whyte point out, desire is too powerful a motivator to ignore. We have all spent too much time doing what we think others want us to do, rather than what we want to do.

In working with all types of clients and situations, I have found that almost anything is attainable if you can conceive of and express it. A few people accomplish this naturally or intuitively, but most of us need a strategy and a game plan for making it happen.

ADOPT THE SELF-BRAND MIND-SET

Each of us is unique, with a mind, strengths, and experiences that are powerful self-brand assets. Anything that you have ever done or thought about could be an asset. If you think it is an asset, it is. If you see it as a stepping-stone to your self-brand goal, it is. If you see it as a career buster, it is.

> *The glass will show thee how thy beauties wear,*
> *the dial who thy precious minutes waste.*
>
> **William Shakespeare**
> *Sonnet 77*

> **SELF-BRANDING**: Self-branding is more than your name, identity, and image. It is everything you do to differentiate and market yourself, such as your messages, self-presentation, and marketing tactics.

Few of us have been taught to think of ourselves in terms of being a *brand*, as something that can be looked at in different ways, developed into a winning brand, and marketed so that we may achieve our full potential.

Few have learned how to rebrand ourselves to stand for something that is in demand rather than something that is no longer in vogue. We don't know how to create positive perceptions of ourselves.

Nor have many of us been taught that we are capable of defining and molding our jobs. We can even create careers and career paths that we feel passionate about.

It's not that ability and performance aren't important. They are. But a talented, hardworking person won't do as well as a well-branded, talented, hardworking person. Effective branding will tip perceptions in your favor and bring greater success.

BREAK THE DEPENDENCY HABIT

We can no longer count on a career at one company. That was your father's Oldsmobile. And now, Oldsmobile is gone altogether!

We will not only have multiple jobs in our lifetimes; we will have multiple careers.

Men at times are masters of their fates.

William Shakespeare
Julius Caesar (I, 2)

> Companies focus on what's good for their bottom line. Not
> what's good for your bottom line.

Companies merge and split up. There are downsizings and upsizings. The boss who hired you moves on. People get into trouble and point fingers at others. Technology and global economies have made outsourcing of jobs possible in ways never imagined just a few years ago. And managerial jobs are not immune.

With these kinds of changes the norm, you can't count on your company to keep you on the payroll. Even when things are going well, conditions can change quickly. You need to control your destiny.

That's why this book contains a number of brainstormers like the one on the opposite page. As you do each brainstormer, write your responses in the spaces provided in cursive handwriting. Why? You'll likely find that writing in cursive engages the brain and helps you think of more ideas.

When you think as if you were a brand, your goal is to prosper, not just survive. Like any brand manager, you must change your strategy and tactics when the marketplace dynamics change. You look for new opportunities and needs for which *your* brand is the solution.

TAKE CHARGE OF YOUR BRAND, OR SOMEONE ELSE WILL

Self-branding is about making the most of what you've got. It's about daring to put forth a different idea. It's about responding to changes in the marketplace.

Many of us keep doing the same things long after they are not working anymore. Self-branding is about playing an active role in your career and life and learning how to position and market yourself to maximum advantage.

After all, it's a myth to think that you'll be rewarded solely on the basis of your hard work. And if you don't brand yourself, someone else will. Chances are that their brand description won't be quite what you have in mind, as my client Kate found out.

‹‹ BRAINSTORMER ››

Who's Looking Out for You?

Envision the following scenario: One day, a major catastrophe occurs at your company headquarters, causing fear and uncertainty. The economy sours, and your company's sales plummet. Then, your boss walks into your office and says, "Sorry, I have some bad news for you. We have to downsize and you're job is being eliminated."

The job market is dreadful, particularly in your industry and geographic area. What do you do now?

Kate had been with a large food company for 10 years and was working hard running a good-size department. Unlike colleagues with similar responsibilities who had been rewarded with promotions to vice president, Kate languished at the senior director level. So why the disparity?

> *Defer no time,*
> *Delays have dangerous ends.*
>
> **William Shakespeare**
> *Henry VI, Part One* (III, 2)

We all have seen it happen: similar staff and responsibilities, but different compensation and title.

Kate got an inkling of the reason when she was at a large corporate meeting. The executive vice president introduced her to a new recruit as "Kate, the person who handles promotions for Brand X."

Well, that had been true several years and several promotions ago, when she was a junior employee, yet that was where her brand was stuck in management's consciousness. Her personal brand was so weak that she was subject to whatever foolish, unproductive brand others associated with her.

Kate desperately needed to rebrand herself as a leader in the company. She took a range of actions aimed at increasing her visibility and changing the perception that her key target markets, her boss and senior executives, had of her.

For starters, she volunteered for a high-profile, strategic project and joined the team that would be making the presentation to senior management. The project gave her a platform for collaborating with executives at her level and above, people with whom she did not interact in her normal job routine.

Kate had to shift her brand from that of assistant to senior management, who *organizes* the material, to that of senior management, who *own* the material.

Her focus is now on capturing the brand she desires. With a change in mind-set, so that she sees herself as a self-brand and not as an employee, Kate is on her way to being branded for success.

COULD SELF-BRANDING HELP YOU?

Self-branding is for people who are smart and good at what they do but not good at branding themselves effectively. It is for people who have come to realize that they need to take control of their identities. They can't rely on luck or other people or situations.

It is for people who want to do and achieve more, people who have a problem (job loss, etc.), and people who want to reinvent themselves for a second act.

All of these people have come to realize that there is no security in a job—any job. Security lies in your ability to take charge. It lies in your ability to brand yourself successfully and think in terms of market needs. Security lies in your ability to respond to change and benefit from it

SELF-BRAND MIND-SET	VS. EMPLOYEE MIND-SET
Working for yourself	Working for boss
Internal security	External security
Marketing plan	Résumé
Markets	Clients, co-workers, management
Differentiating	Fitting in
Strategy	Hard work
Relationships	Transactions
Network	Solo
Long-term	Short-term
Planning	Reacting
Sound bites	Business jargon
Packaging	Clothes
Visibility	Low profile
Self-measurement	Performance review

rather than hide from it. Security lies in your ability to develop a strategy and a game plan.

Security lies in you.

TAKE ACTION—NOW

The bottom line is, branding provides a valuable tool for leveraging the asset that is you. But it is a powerless tool unless you act. See the box on the following page for my list of the top 10 self-branding actions you can take and that we will explore in the chapters that follow.

The first secret of personal branding is that the magic is in you. You can take charge and harness your passion and drive. Become emotionally and intellectually engaged in your professional and life journeys. Start to create your own luck. Seek your own solutions.

> *Why, then the world's mine oyster!*
>
> **William Shakespeare**
> *The Merry Wives of Windsor* **(II, 2)**

The more self-reliant you are, the more luck and solutions you will find. Start developing options for yourself rather than waiting for them. A surge in self-esteem is one unexpected benefit of finding your own solutions to your situation. And stronger self-esteem will make it easier for you to enact them.

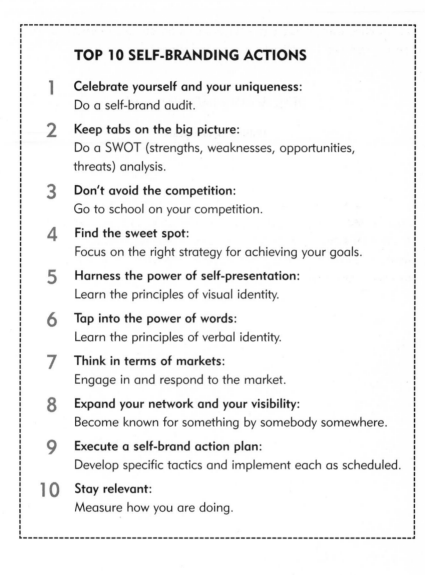

TOP 10 SELF-BRANDING ACTIONS

1   **Celebrate yourself and your uniqueness:**
    Do a self-brand audit.

2   **Keep tabs on the big picture:**
    Do a SWOT (strengths, weaknesses, opportunities,
    threats) analysis.

3   **Don't avoid the competition:**
    Go to school on your competition.

4   **Find the sweet spot:**
    Focus on the right strategy for achieving your goals.

5   **Harness the power of self-presentation:**
    Learn the principles of visual identity.

6   **Tap into the power of words:**
    Learn the principles of verbal identity.

7   **Think in terms of markets:**
    Engage in and respond to the market.

8   **Expand your network and your visibility:**
    Become known for something by somebody somewhere.

9   **Execute a self-brand action plan:**
    Develop specific tactics and implement each as scheduled.

10 **Stay relevant:**
    Measure how you are doing.

<< IN A NUTSHELL >>

The first secret of self-brands:

That person in the mirror

is the only one you can rely on.

But that's not sad.

It's powerful.

THINK DIFFERENT TO BECOME A BRAND APART

> *This above all, To thine ownself be true.*
>
> **William Shakespeare**
> *Hamlet* **(I, 3)**

The cardinal rule of branding is "Be different." Copying is imitation.

When you copy, you're not authentic. You are a generic version of a name brand.

You'll be viewed as a B player. And you'll always be playing the catch-up game.

You should build your professional identity around your authenticity: who you are and what you can be, not who you want to be like or who others want you to be. You need to find out what's different about you and your abilities. And capitalize on it.

Best of all, when you build off your strengths and desires, you'll be enthusiastic. You'll be able to indulge your passions. You'll also find that when you accept who you are, others will, too.

MAKE YOUR BRAND A STANDOUT

Having a different idea for your brand is powerful. It will position you apart from the crowd. There are many people competing with you, for your job, your opportunity, your money, your ____. That's why your self-brand must make you stand out from your competitors in the minds of your prospects.

Brand managers spend a lot of time delineating differences: different benefits, different look, different message, different target audience. To determine their different idea, marketers do a *brand audit*, a detailed study of the brand and its competitors. What they are creating is a distinct *brand strategy*, explaining what their brand has to offer that competing brands don't.

> *And say to all the world, "This was a man."*
>
> **William Shakespeare**
> *Julius Caesar* **(V, 5)**

Many people shortchange themselves when it comes to targeting their own different ideas and the benefits to their target markets. They are too busy working hard, but that is not the same as working smart. Don't be one of them.

FIND YOUR UNIQUE SELLING PROPOSITION

When you don't differentiate yourself, people won't have a reason to choose you, as my client Alexandra found out. An executive coach who had been in business for more than 10 years, Alexandra had a marketing brochure and a fancy logo but no different idea. After I read her brochure, all I could remember as a takeaway message was "executive coach who works with all kinds of people and all kinds of problems."

UNIQUE SELLING PROPOSITION (USP): The big idea that brands are always searching for—a USP will give them a compelling value proposition with the target audience.

A lot of entrepreneurs make this mistake. They want to cast a wide net so that they won't miss any business.

However, the opposite usually occurs. They don't get much business because people don't have anything to sink their teeth into. Alexandra offered no reason for someone to choose her and gave no sense of the *kind* of client she was best suited to help.

MAKE A DIFFERENT BRAND PROMISE

We got our brand insight when I asked Alexandra, "What kind of client are you really good with?"

She said, "Believe it or not, I enjoy working with really difficult people. For some reason, I'm good at it. Companies have hired me to work with abusive or impossible managers—you know, the kind that are featured in books like *How to Work for a Jerk*."

Why do companies even bother trying to rehabilitate these people? you might wonder.

The reason is pure and simple: performance. Because they are talented and produce results, companies often want to keep them. But companies need to get these difficult managers to change their behavior or there will be mutiny in the enterprise.

"Are there enough people like that to build a coaching business around?" I asked Alexandra.

"Sure, tons," she assured me. "Plus I'm also good with the stressed-out people who have to work with these difficult people. I've developed methods for helping people cope with impossible bosses and clients so that they are able to control the situation better."

Eureka! We had our different brand promise.

With her focus on difficult managers and the people who work for them, Alexandra had a point of difference and a USP on which to build her self-brand and company brand. She had a public relations platform for pitching reporters doing stories on how to cope with an abusive boss or a difficult client.

Alexandra's different brand strategy also became a way of being memorable and staying at the top of everyone's mind. And as we know, *out of mind* is *out of work*.

ASK "WHY?" "WHAT IF?" "HOW ABOUT?"

As the great Yogi (Yogi Berra, that is) said, "You can observe a lot just by watching."

While you look for ideas for a self-brand strategy, observe what attracts your attention amid all the competing messages that bombard you each day. Once you start looking, you'll find that everything communicates. Branding lessons are everywhere.

Start observing what's working and what isn't. Do it for your company, industry, job. For instance, what has never been questioned in your industry, business, or department? Why not? What would happen if it were? What "rules" of this industry (or company) can be broken? What's missing? How can that lead to an opportunity for you? As the marketing axiom goes, you want to be the kind of market researcher who looks at what everyone else looks at and sees something different.

> *Knowledge, the wing wherewith we fly to heaven.*
>
> **William Shakespeare**
> *Henry VI, Part Two* **(IV, 7)**

Look at people who brand themselves well. What are their strong attributes? What makes them special?

Look at yourself. If you were a competitor, how would you critique yourself? How do your attributes compare with those your company prizes? (Don't just ask yourself these questions; answer them.)

Another way to go about exploring possibilities for yourself is to begin with the end in mind and work backward, as the next brainstormer shows.

Whenever you see someone lead a successful project or give an exciting presentation, ask yourself what made it so special. Whenever you see someone doing something novel and find yourself saying, "Gee, that was a great idea," think about how you might put your spin on it.

You can get self-branding ideas every day just by following stories in the media. If you're in business, read business publications like the *Wall Street Journal* or *Fortune* for success stories and cautionary tales. Or read magazines like the *New Yorker* or the *Atlantic* for thoughtful articles on opinion leaders and issues of the day.

‹‹ BRAINSTORMER ››

Imagining the Outcome First

Think in terms of the outcome you want and work backward. Let's say, for example, that you want to dramatically increase your salary. Here's how you might go about it. Ask yourself the following questions.

What would make an employer double your salary?

What do you need to have in your self-brand profile that you don't have now?

Watch how people present themselves and their ideas on television talk shows. Even the media with its cult of celebrities could be a source of inspiration.

START WITH A HYPOTHESIS

When you first begin on your self-branding journey, don't get muddled by all the "facts" as you analyze your brand and the market.

Begin by tapping into your gut. What does your intuition tell you about your identity and lifework? The best ideas and strategies often come through brainstorming and hypothesizing before we do any research. Deep down, we already know the answer.

The *initial hypothesis* is a technique that some management consultants use with great success. Yes, you actually can come up with the

> **SELF-BRAND HYPOTHESIS:** Don't neglect to consult your intuition before you do research and formal analysis. An "ignorant" idea or hunch may be more insightful and valuable than a labored study of the situation.

answers to your personal, business, or marketing problem before all the careful research studies and analysis get in the way and muddle your vision.

The reason is simple. An initial hypothesis based on hunches and intuition often has the greatest insight into a problem. And that insight is often the solution to your self-branding, or personal, or any other problem.

Your hunch is often as accurate as a solution developed from careful study and analysis and may be more meaningful as well. In preparing to develop an initial hypothesis for a new piece of business or a brand assignment, a branding firm usually puts together a small, diverse team. The team includes people who are experts in the brand category and people who have little or no knowledge about the issue. (Nonexperts don't have the baggage that can hinder fresh insight.)

You can do the same. You are the expert on the brand You. You can do the self-brand hypothesis session yourself or even invite some friends over to brainstorm with you.

If you are doing your initial hypothesis solo, go to a quiet place where you can let your thoughts roam as you explore your thoughts. If you put together a group, choose people you think are insightful, and mix it up so that you have both hard and soft thinking skills. In either case, the brainstormer on the following page will help guide your thinking.

As you brainstorm, you may discover some new insights or even a career path or business strategy that really pans out for you. It happens all the time.

The rule for brainstorming is "No idea is a bad idea." Censoring causes people to shut down their creative juices. Anyway, it often happens that a so-called dumb idea spurs you to think of ways to debunk it. That will help sharpen your focus.

‹‹ BRAINSTORMER ››

Developing Your Hypothesis

Here are some questions to prod your hypothetical thinking.

What's different, special, unusual, or weird about the brand You?

If you were managing this brand, where would you take it in five years?

What should you be doing to make meaning in the world?

What is the key piece of advice you would give this brand?

You might even want to really get into the spirit of it and create a war-room atmosphere as ad agencies do and post ideas on large sheets of paper on the wall. This will help you evaluate the various hypotheses. Often, the right solution will jump out from the pack.

THE SWOT ANALYSIS

One of the first things marketers do is conduct a *brand audit*. Marketers analyze a brand by studying its strengths, weaknesses, opportunities, and threats (SWOT). This is just plain common sense. The SWOT analysis is an intensive look at your strengths and weaknesses in a real-world framework. It will help you focus on your strengths and deflect your weaknesses. It will help you zero in on opportunities and threats on your professional horizon, even uncover hidden information.

As a self-brand strategist, you must always be relevant and find new opportunities. We spend too much of our time following so many rules or simply plodding ahead that we don't see the opportunity. Doing a periodic SWOT analysis will keep you on track.

Strengths and Weaknesses

"Strengths" and "weaknesses," the first two areas, deal with you.

Think of strengths as assets that could be links to your success. Assets are areas you can build on, and practically anything could be an asset. Start with skills, experience, and accomplishments. What parts of your job are fun to do?

Then expand the list to include personality traits. Expand it further to include anyone you have known or even met, and anything that you have explored or been interested in. The hidden assets or self-taught skills that come up through probing often hold the key.

Weaknesses are areas to avoid, since you are not on solid ground there. However, some weaknesses, such as communication skills and networking, may be areas to target for development, as they are integral to your life strategy.

Opportunities and Threats

The "opportunities" and "threats" sections in the SWOT analysis deal with things that could affect you in the future. What is going on that could dramatically change things? What is not working well? Business is dynamic, so there is always movement and change. (Look at the current threats to the American job market outlined in *The World Is Flat* by Thomas Friedman.) Change always creates new opportunities and new threats.

For example, if you're in school, you need to start anticipating the job market in the fields you are studying. Some areas will offer tons of growth and financial rewards, while others will be tough slogging. In the 1990s, Wall Street and high technology were the hot spots, and many people rode that wave to fame and fortune. You need to find the best wave to ride for your future.

If you have a job, you need to keep tabs on what is taking place that could threaten your livelihood in the future, whether it's the economy, your industry, or your company. And you want to keep your sights on the new opportunities that any change will bring about. The SWOT analysis will help you find the link between a market opportunity and your strengths and desires.

The SWOT analysis is also helpful in analyzing a potential new job or company. Many people who switch don't succeed in their new jobs.

It's important to do your homework before you get romanced in the job interview process. The culture has to be a good fit for you. How healthy is the company or group you'll be joining? Some managers hire people to prop up a department or division that is already on life support. Unfortunately, they neglect to warn the job candidate that the position is a turnaround situation. Too many people find out the hard way.

Every job you take will either increase or decrease the value of your self-brand. The SWOT brainstormer on the following page will help you plot the right moves.

TURN THE SWOT ANALYSIS UP A NOTCH

The overriding goal of the SWOT analysis is to find links between your strengths and new market opportunities. You want to develop strategies that will be advantageous to you in terms of the market's future direction.

When you have completed the SWOT brainstormer, if you're like most people, you will have a long list of strengths and weaknesses. You'll probably have a smaller list of future opportunities with some threats looming on the horizon.

It's often smart to start with the list of opportunities and then review your strengths and assets. After that, you should be able to identify the ones that best position you to take advantage of those opportunities. For example, choose the two or three most critical opportunities that suit the future you see for yourself. Then, pick the strengths that play into each opportunity.

I brainstormed in a similar way when I started my company, SelfBrand. I wanted to do something entrepreneurial after a long career working for others. I saw an opportunity to bring my strategic branding approach to companies as a brand strategist. But I also saw an opportunity to do something more novel—to take the branding process used in the commercial world and apply it to people so that they could achieve their potential in career and personal growth.

<< BRAINSTORMER >>

Doing the SWOT Analysis

1. Strengths: Write down anything that you are good at and love to do. Write down what your boss, clients, or colleagues give you high marks on. (It may or may not be true, but it's how you're currently perceived.)

2. Weaknesses: Write down what you're terrible at and hate to do, or what your boss and friends criticize you for.

3. Opportunities: This is wide open. Write down anything that could be an opportunity for you. A key is to look for unmet or unsatisfied needs in your company or business on which you could capitalize.

4. Threats: Write down what keeps you awake at night about yourself or your career or business, whether real or imagined.

Extra credit: Circle the top two or three critical factors in each category. Look for the intersection of a new market opportunity and your strengths and assets. Brainstorm the possibilities.

I knew that in the current world of work, many people would need self-branding skills in order to move from job to job and rebrand themselves for wholly new careers. More people will become entrepreneurs and they will need to develop a strong self-brand in tandem with a company brand.

I realized that people need to think of their careers as a strategic and creative process similar to the branding process. Plus, my clients could learn from all the mistakes that I had made along the way!

CHOOSE AN "ENEMY"

You'll want to look at another page from the branding playbook: *competitive analysis.*

Go to school on your competition. A competitor is anyone who is pursuing the same goal or target market that you are pursuing.

Respect your competitors, but don't be afraid of them. Be different from them. Analyze them. (If you can analyze them, you can be better than them.)

Smart marketers think in terms of *choosing an enemy* to position their brands against. Rather than viewing competition as a negative thing, flip it. View competitors' attributes as they highlight your strengths and advantages: Position your strengths against their weaknesses, and reposition their strengths as less important attributes.

For example, Leonardo da Vinci positioned his younger rival Michelangelo as a mere sculptor, not a painter like himself. He even tried to brand Michelangelo as a technician, who looked like a "baker" with white marble dust on his clothes, rather than an artist.

Of course, Leonardo's branding attempt didn't stick. Michelangelo went on to paint the ceiling of the Sistine Chapel. His dynamic, muscular style of painting was influenced by his background as a sculptor and immediately became the talk of Rome. There was no doubt that Michelangelo's brand footprint was quite big enough to encompass painter and sculptor.

Competition also means that your field is attractive and lucrative. After all, if it weren't, why would people want to be part of it? Your status is elevated and worth more because competition has created a lot of interest.

‹‹ BRAINSTORMER ››

Positioning Competitors

Describe each competitor in one positive word. Think of it as the competitor's **keyword**.

Describe each competitor in one negative word. This is the competitor's main weakness or **strike point**.

What do you have to offer that they don't? This is your **value proposition**.

Now, sell your value proposition against your key competitor— your "enemy."

Marketers study their brand competitors by looking at a competitive analysis of product features, television commercials and print ads, market research studies, and the like. What can you do to study your competitors? You can always start by Googling them to see what comes up. Use the brainstormer above to position and define your competitors.

FIND YOUR DIFFERENT IDEA

Branding is a competition. It's a competition over what you stand for versus what someone else stands for. It's a competition over ideas.

In self-branding, you're searching for your different idea, a different idea that resonates with your target market. You're searching for a different idea that will help you compete and win.

> *It is the mind that makes the body rich.*
>
> **William Shakespeare**
> *Taming of the Shrew* **(IV, 3)**

The way to do well is to not run with the herd. You must look at yourself as a brand in a competitive marketplace. Find the advantage of your different idea.

Just as brands always have to be tweaked to stay relevant, so do you. After all, the goal of making yourself a relevant self-brand is to connect with other people and to be able to offer them something.

So don't neglect what's different and authentic about you. It is the most wonderful thing you have to offer the world.

‹‹ IN A NUTSHELL ››

The second secret of self-brands:

Study the market and the competition,

but don't follow the herd.

Find your different idea.

SEARCH FOR THE SWEET SPOT WHERE YOU AND A MARKET OPPORTUNITY MEET

> We know what we are
> but know not what we may be.
>
> **William Shakespeare**
> *Hamlet* (I, 5)

In self-branding, you are looking for the sweet spot: the intersection of a good idea and a market need that you can satisfy.

For most people, the problem with finding the sweet spot is not a lack of ideas and information but too many competing ideas and too much information. The hard part is figuring out which things are important and which are worthless.

Each person's situation is unique, but the self-branding process involves analyzing the facts in the marketplace and looking at ideas and options. But it also involves trusting your instincts and tapping into your intuition as you mold your future. You must use both your brains and your gut instincts as you focus your brand.

FOLLOW YOUR INSTINCTS

Handsome and athletic, Anthony cut an impressive figure when we met. It was quite a contrast from our phone conversation a week earlier. Then, an emotional Anthony had described being laid off six months earlier by an elite Wall Street firm and his very frustrating job hunt.

Up until that day, Anthony had led what would seem to many to be a fairy-tale existence. He attended top schools and then landed a plum job as an analyst with a Wall Street investment bank.

Life was sweet for several years, until his specialty, merger and acquisitions advisory work in the telecommunications industry, went sour. And he was out on the street.

Diligent professional that he is, Anthony had spent the past six months meeting recruiters, sending out résumés, and commiserating with other newly unemployed investment bankers. Like them, he was looking for a job at an investment bank or in a corporate finance department. The problem: a dead job market and lots of job hunters with MBAs on the loose.

> **If you don't stand for something relevant to the marketplace, you have no value.**

My jaw dropped when I asked Anthony where he would like to see himself professionally in five years. His answer had almost no relationship to what he was doing now or what he was looking for.

Anthony's childhood dream was to be an entrepreneur just as his grandfather had been years ago in India. His new twist: He wanted to develop his own business advising Western companies on increasing business with the new moneyed class in India.

"Well, if that's where you want to go, you'll never get there by looking for a job like the one you had in telecommunications," I told him. "You'll have to do different things from what you are doing now if that's where you want to end up."

Yes, change can be scary. But sometimes it's scarier not to change.

CREATE PROOF POINTS

Job number one for Anthony was to develop a self-brand strategy and action plan that would get him pointed in the right direction.

Our first problem was Anthony's glaring lack of the credentials necessary to achieve his dreams. We needed *proof points* to demonstrate that he could be successful doing business in India and that he understood the affluent Indian market. We hypothesized that his first order of business was to find employment with a Western firm that wanted to develop the new affluent market in India.

Anthony was in a classic catch-22 situation. He couldn't get such a job without experience, and he couldn't get experience without the job. We needed to create *perceptual links* between what he had been doing and what he wanted to do so that he could move forward.

> *Nothing will come of nothing.*
>
> **William Shakespeare**
> *King Lear* (I, 1)

To provide the perceptual links of experience and understanding of the Indian market, we hit upon a novel solution. We developed a pilot research study to measure awareness of U.S. brands among the newly wealthy in India.

Ad agencies often field a pilot research study when pitching a piece of business. They hope that the insights gained from the research will give them a strategic advantage in the new business process. It is also a tactic that you can use successfully, particularly in new geographic markets and customer segments or for radically new product areas. And it can be done affordably in smaller markets or even as a do-it-yourself project over the Internet. Don't position it as full-blown research but as a *pilot* study.

It may be more difficult to implement a pilot study for mature industries unless you come up with a new angle because there is already so much information on those markets. But the opposite is true of newer markets, like Anthony's, because not much information is available.

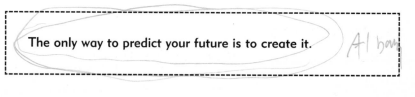

The only way to predict your future is to create it.

THINK BIG

Then, Anthony started creating his own luck. Through networking, he located a businessman who wanted to explore the prospect of developing a business in India. He agreed not only to fund the study but to pay Anthony's travel expenses, too.

Next, we drafted letters to key Western companies—all the companies on Anthony's list of desirable places to work. In the letters, we said that Anthony was off to conduct a pilot research study of the newly wealthy consumer market in India and was including their brand in the study. Anthony offered to meet with them to share his findings after he completed the study.

Were there some dead ends? Sure. But so what?

Bottom line: the strategy worked. Of the first 12 companies that received his letter, 9 responded, a truly astounding rate. It was clearly the right strategy at the right time. He even booked 6 appointments with senior executives at target companies before he left.

In India, Anthony used the research study he was conducting as a door opener both with Western firms and with Indian nationals involved in sales and marketing, public relations, events planning, and market research.

> *Self-love my liege is not so vile a sin as self-neglecting.*
>
> **William Shakespeare**
> *King Henry V* (II, 4)

When Anthony returned to the United States, he had a busy calendar. In follow-up meetings and interviews with senior executives, he successfully positioned himself as a rare bird—a global business executive who could bridge East and West. He was a savvy citizen of the West and also a person of Indian heritage who could speak local languages and forge strong ties.

UNCOVER HIDDEN ASSETS

Anthony had another asset, which he didn't see as valuable at first.

His grandfather's name and business reputation were unique assets. Even though his grandfather was no longer alive, his business reputation in India gave Anthony a compelling and memorable story to tell and leverage wherever he went.

In India, Anthony's family heritage helped him meet lots of people in marketing, retailing, public relations, and manufacturing. In the West, Anthony made a point of mentioning that he came from a family with an established business name in India. Family heritage is important in many areas of the world and could help open doors for Western companies.

Anthony's heritage gave him an enormous advantage. But, even without it, his strategy would still have worked. After all, many Western companies had set up appointments for interviews on the basis of his initial letter outlining his proposed pilot study.

Anthony's transformation was just as powerful as anything you'd see on *Extreme Makeovers*. Potential employers and business contacts now saw him in a completely different way.

Once he had a few big-name interviews under his belt, Anthony leveraged those appointments to garner meetings with other Western manufacturers. He was on his way to reaching his dream. Anthony had found the *sweet spot* where his abilities and desires intersected with a real need in the marketplace. The suggestions and questions in the brainstormer on the following page will help you recognize your dream.

MEET CHANGE WITH CHANGE

When situations change, *you* must change if you intend to succeed.

Kayla had an extensive background in marketing and sales in the technology industry. When she first called me, the rumor mill at the company where she worked was in high gear. Reports were starting to appear in the press that another company was going to buy her company.

Like just about everyone else in her department, Kayla was worried about a merger and job cuts. She was like a deer caught in the headlights. She wasn't getting much work done on the job, and she wasn't taking much action about her situation on the outside either—that is, until the merger deal was announced two weeks later.

> *Sweet are the uses of adversity.*
>
> **William Shakespeare**
> *As You Like It* (II, 1)

‹‹ BRAINSTORMER ››

What If?

Go to a quiet place where you can let your thoughts roam as you answer these questions. Follow your instincts.

What are you really passionate about?

What's your dream job? What would you do if you knew you couldn't fail?

What is missing from your current life that you must have going forward?

What could you do tomorrow to get started?

When Kayla and I did the SWOT analysis, we spent a lot of time looking at the changes taking place in the technology industry, especially the opportunities and threats part of the analysis. Even though the merger was being billed in the press as a merger of equals, we knew that some employees would survive and others wouldn't. We knew that all bets were off in terms of job security.

Change seemed inevitable. The consolidation train was leaving the station, and lots of companies were jumping on it. So moving to another company wouldn't necessarily increase Kayla's immunity to a merger or potential job loss.

Kayla needed a strategy for ending her paralysis and developing options for her future. Rather than sit around and worry about where the ax was going to fall next, Kayla took action.

NICHE YOUR SELF-BRAND

The key was *focus*. Rather than position Kayla as the marketing generalist that she was, we narrowed our focus to an area that allowed her to demonstrate a touch of nonpareil excellence.

We zeroed in on loyalty marketing: one-to-one marketing designed to create long-term relationships with a company's best customers. Loyalty marketing was a new area in which Kayla had done some exciting and successful projects. She hypothesized that customer loyalty would be even more important in the future as everyone vied for the same customer, particularly the young high-tech consumer that was her specialty. We thought loyalty marketing was the sweet spot for Kayla given our take on market needs and trends.

Narrow focus goes against the grain for most people. They think that the broader their job description, the better off they will be. So most of Kayla's colleagues were positioning themselves as marketing generalists with a long list of capabilities.

Kayla had a broad background in marketing, too; but marketing generalists were becoming a commodity.

The acquiring company was weak in the emerging area of loyalty marketing, and this was an important factor in our decision. (Kayla had done her competitive analysis.)

> **Look for a market niche where there are no entrenched competitors.**

DRAMATIZE YOUR RÉSUMÉ

Kayla's résumé was a laundry list of skills and job experience. There was no focus or message. Her résumé was full of business jargon and bland descriptions and looked downright forbidding in terms of layout. It was not a self-branding document.

The first thing I wanted Kayla to do was to shift from the idea of her résumé as job history to her résumé as an ad for brand Kayla. She needed to develop a résumé that was strategically focused and interesting, like a good ad. To do that, we put a headline positioning Kayla at the top of the résumé. Under her name, we put the following line: Loyalty Marketing—The Fickle Twenty-Something Tech Consumer— Innovative Customer-Retention Programs. We developed her self-brand message in a profile paragraph set right underneath and used the body of the résumé to tell a story of innovative projects tied into clear-cut results and customer reaction.

All the change taking place in the technology field was obvious, but we needed to put Kayla on the winning side of the change with new ideas and solutions for potential employers.

The focus of Kayla's message was her innovative loyalty marketing programs for the 18- to 24-year-old, tech-oriented market. We wanted potential employers (including the new management that came with the merger) to know that Kayla had a lock on how these consumers think and act. We linked the marketing initiatives she had spearheaded that were outside the loyalty marketing area around core ideas related to loyalty marketing and showed how they increased customer life, frequency, and profits.

The final shift Kayla needed to make was to create a visually and verbally memorable résumé. The layout should look inviting, and the copy should capture readers' attention and compel them to read more.

Most résumés list accomplishments in the most general way. A long list of skills and responsibilities presented in vague language doesn't get noticed. A résumé that sells you must focus on a message and use action words to bring your self-brand story to life.

CASCADE YOUR ACHIEVEMENTS

A clever way to set your résumé apart from the pack is to place a one- or two-page *achievement addendum* at the back. It's a must for a senior executive but can benefit everyone; it's often the clincher in the sale.

An achievement addendum is the something more that sets you apart and encourages an employer to choose you and not the other guy. (And something more is mandatory in a tough job market.)

‹‹ BRAINSTORMER ››

Creating an Achievement Addendum

Think of any project to which you contributed in an important way at work or in your community.

What challenge did you face?

How did you approach the project in an innovative way?

Were there any novel solutions or unexpected problems?

What actions did you take?

What were the quantifiable results? The emotional results?

Describe the results as visually and vividly as possible.

An achievement addendum allows you to showcase the most powerful parts of your personal story with more detail and excitement. Use a case study format such as problem, solution, results or challenge, action, and accomplishment.

Tell the story of the project or initiative so that people can participate in the challenge and the steps you took to succeed. Use the active voice and action words and describe specifics as if you were telling a colleague about the project. Avoid business or technical jargon.

If you worked on an important project outside the office—in your community or with a political campaign, for example—the achievement addendum is a great place to capitalize on it. The next brainstormer will help you get started.

CREATE ENDORSEMENT BUZZ

Great résumés have another extra, a surprise element that makes the reader want to learn more about the person. In order to separate Kayla's résumé further from the pack, we needed to create a different *brand experience* for people who came in contact with her résumé. We took a tactic from the advertising playbook and used *customer testimonials.*

Of course, Kayla didn't have customers in the traditional sense, but she did have two former bosses, a manager, and several clients who were happy with projects she had spearheaded. We put together case studies of these projects in the achievement addendum and featured a quote from a former boss or client at the top of each one. One of her former bosses had moved on to a prominent job, and we placed his "celebrity" endorsement first.

These endorsements of Kayla's abilities created buzz and helped her score more interviews. It allowed her to showcase her successes through someone else's words.

If you say it, it's bragging.

If your boss or colleague says it, it's expert testimony.

The achievement addendum gave Kayla a reason to call up former colleagues, not to ask for a job lead, but to ask for a quote for her addendum. (In the course of their conversations, however, these people often came up with suggestions for people Kayla could meet with.)

DAZZLE THE INTERVIEWER

Kayla, like most people, always went into a job interview feeling power-less. She boned up on possible questions and the company itself and went to the meeting expecting a formal interview.

Wrong, wrong, wrong! With that kind of mind-set, it will be hard to feel genuine and comfortable in your own skin. You'll be too worried about how you are going to answer the questions. What you need to do is take control. Create a more relaxed experience so that a conversation takes place. You want to make the meeting more informal and conversational as quickly as possible.

The first impression you create is critical. The way you look, enter the room, and explain yourself in the first 30 seconds will make or break you. You must prepare your *elevator speech:* a pithy story about yourself that you could tell in the length of time it takes to travel several floors in an elevator. It should be an interesting narrative that positions you and dramatizes the benefit you bring to a project or a company. Practice it out loud. See the brainstormer on the following page to get you started.

You should also be able to tell interesting stories about your professional adventures. Think in terms of cascading your message and capabilities around various themes, such as the following:

‹‹ BRAINSTORMER ››

Creating Your 30 Seconds

Set a timer for 30 seconds. Practice your self-brand opener. What hooks, connections, or stories can you add that will make your opening more powerful and relevant? Write your response in the space below.

> Rags to riches
> The turning point
> Against all odds
> Hero to my client

TURN THE TABLES

As a self-brander, you have your agenda too. So as soon as you can, ask *them* questions. Interview them. And *listen* more than you talk.

The more an interviewer talks, the more interested in you the interviewer will be.

It is a very powerful tactic, because if you work a series of questions into the conversation, you immediately level the playing field.

In place of a one-way dialogue and a one-way relationship, you've created a two-way dialogue and a two-way relationship.

Ask about key initiatives and projects. You want to know more about the culture. When you take this approach (in a friendly way), you will come across as a person with options. You'll find that your worth will skyrocket in the mind of the interviewer. Likewise, if you try to sell yourself too hard or want quick feedback on how you stack up compared to the other candidates, your value will plummet.

Ask questions and listen. Listening is an art. You'll create a great impression and learn a lot at the same time. When you listen rather than talk, you flatter your audience. Listening says that you think the other person is smart and worth listening to.

> *I hear, yet say not much, hear the more.*
>
> **William Shakespeare**
> ***Much Ado About Nothing* (III, 2)**

Since you're not trying so hard to *sell yourself* in the interview, what usually happens, as Kayla found out, is that the interviewer starts to sell you on the company and the job. When an interviewer starts to feel comfortable, she might even share war stories about the company or industry. When the balance of power between two people is more equal, it is much more likely to result in a job offer.

When you create more dialogue in an interview situation, you come across as confident and not needy. You give the impression of a person with options who's not just going to grab the first thing but is looking for the right thing.

It's a fact of branding that people want something all the more when they think it is not so easy to get. (Why do you think luxury goods manufacturers produce small lots so that there are waiting lists?) You want to create the perception that you are a brand that is in demand, too, even if you would give your first-born for the job. Always remember that people will buy because they want to, not because they're being sold.

THINK AND ACT SMART

There is no one *right* brand identity, benefit, or message, although some will be much more successful for you than the others will. Find the things about you that are remarkable enough to meet real needs in the marketplace. Focus on your different idea, create a different brand experience, but above all, do something.

> *Strike now or else the iron cools.*
>
> **William Shakespeare**
> *Henry IV, Part Three* (V, 1)

Avoid the urge to procrastinate or talk yourself out of doing something because you're not ready yet. The best and only time to do something is the present.

We all are dealt different hands in life. Your hand is all good as long as you use it in the right way.

Make use of everything. You have experiences; these are brand assets. You have a point of view; that too is an asset. Make the best use of the assets and resources you have and realize that we all have hidden assets that we need to uncover.

Successful people often make use of what others view as worthless or insignificant. Be one of them.

‹‹ IN A NUTSHELL ››

The third secret of self-brands:

Look for the sweet spot.

Uncover hidden assets that meet a real market need:

You—fresh, unique, powerful.

4

FIND A GREAT SELF-BRAND STRATEGY TO GET GREAT RESULTS

> *Some are born great. Some achieve greatness.*
> *Some have greatness thrust upon them.*
>
> **William Shakespeare**
> *Twelfth Night* **(II, 3)**

Strategy is the brains of branding.

A good self-brand strategy is similar to a brand strategy for a company or a product. Strategy is developing a *winnable position* in the marketplace with a smart game plan and tactics for achieving it.

When you look at the successful people around you, you might notice that they may or may not be the smartest or the most talented, but I'll wager they each had a strategy (whether they called it that).

Smarts and talent are important but overrated. We all know lots of smart and talented people who are not doing well professionally.

Even luck is overrated. Sure, luck helps. But most successful people *create* their own luck. Then they give their stories a more romantic spin by saying it was luck and not hard work that got them there.

Strategy is underrated and much more valuable. As the marketing consultant David Beckwith has stated, "All strategies are not created equal. Terrific strategies and tactics more than beat good ones; they work hundreds of times better."

> **SELF-BRAND STRATEGY:** A crisp positioning statement that defines your "big idea" or unique selling proposition (USP)—what's different and special about you in comparison to others and why it matters.

I agree with Beckwith, but don't wait until you figure out a killer strategy. Get started now. You're ready for strategic development after you've done the research, analyzed the competition, and completed your analysis of strengths, weaknesses, opportunities, and threats (SWOT).

Having a strategy gives you a lot of advantages. Developing a strategy forces you to think, and that in itself will start to give you an advantage over many people. Strategy also compels you to think big picture and long term.

DEVELOP A SELF-BRAND STRATEGY

Your self-brand strategy should be short and focused.

It should be short enough to write on the back of a business card. If you can't say it briefly, your strategy is probably muddled.

Your strategy should dramatize a benefit. And it should be distinctive enough to intrigue people and make them want to know more.

> *Brevity is the soul of wit.*
>
> **William Shakespeare**
> *Hamlet* (II, 2)

The verbal counterpart is the elevator speech. The elevator speech articulates your strategy in a brief, conversational way that you can use when meeting new professional acquaintances or at job interviews and the like.

The ability to articulate what your brand is about is important. After all, if you can't articulate it, how can you expect anyone else to get it? You need to create the focus and the sizzle.

Ad agencies use a simple format for brand strategy statement. They aim for a punchy statement of the *positioning* that sets the brand apart from its competitors. They follow the positioning with *proof points*—concrete examples—or credentials that support the positioning strategy.

Another way of putting together a brand strategy is though analogy. Try to put two different ideas together to express your brand, such as "I'm a cross between _____ and _____," or "I'm like _____ meets _____." For example, Tazo defined the brand strategy for its tea as "Marco Polo meets Merlin."

Here are two examples of self-brand strategies from the client stories in chapter 3.

Anthony's Self-Brand Strategy
Anthony is a rare bird: East meets West.

Here are the credentials Anthony used to support his strategy:

> Dynamic Western-trained business executive with Indian family heritage

> Understands emerging elite class in India through pilot market research study

> Asian business ties through family heritage and research project

Kayla's Self-Brand Strategy
Kayla creates loyalty programs that make young customers stick around.

Here are some of the proof points Kayla used:

> Innovative loyalty marketing initiatives expanded this group's share of wallet by 23 percent last year

> Internet game/competition on the company Website brought in 15,500 new customers and expanded share of spending by existing customers by 28 percent

STRATEGIZE DIFFERENTLY

Truly great self-brand strategies often meet resistance at first as any new idea does.

When you take a different stance, you are, well, different, and that may cause discomfort at first. Your brand strategy might not appeal to everyone, and that might make you uncomfortable.

But if your brand strategy does not have a bit of an edgy quality, it is probably a strategy that a lot of people are using.

Would you have me false to my nature?
Rather, say I plan the man I am.

William Shakespeare
Coriolanus (III, 2)

Remember, if the way you talk about yourself and what you can do doesn't have some sizzle, chances are that people will peg you as a commodity. You have to be intriguing enough to stand out in your category.

BE AUTHENTIC

Your strategy must come out of who you are.

Remember, the sign over the entrance to the Delphic oracle's temple read "Know thyself." You'll never make it by copying someone else's strategy or image. Your quest is to uncover yours.

One way to start is by eliminating what is superfluous, what is not intrinsic to who you are. When Michelangelo carved a statue, he believed that the sculpture was already there in the rough piece of stone. His job was to eliminate all the superfluous stone and reveal the David or Pieta hidden within.

Your job is similar. Eliminate things that are not unique to you. Focus on what is authentic—your human truth—and what resonates with the people you are targeting.

In short, here are the four essentials of a self-brand strategy:

1. *Be different:* Imitation will make you only a B player.

2. *Focus:* Limit yourself to a dozen words or less so you can bore into the essential idea in a quick, punchy way.

3. *Be authentic:* Your strategy must be based on who you are and the assets and experiences you can claim. (Of course, you may create some new experiences.)

4. *Resonate in the market:* If you don't get a reaction in the market-place, go back to the drawing board.

BONE UP ON THE BIG BRANDS

One way to figure out the best self-brand strategy is to look at brand strategies from the commercial world.

Start by devouring good books on individual companies and products. Successful brands always attract analysis. Or read about how brands develop winning strategies. (My favorite marketing authors are Al Ries and Jack Trout, my bosses in my first advertising job.)

Once you start studying the world of commercial branding, you'll see how branding strategies and tactics have lessons for you, too.

Following are 10 positioning strategies from the commercial world that clients have used to build a strong self-brand. Do the brainstormers for each self-brand strategy. Don't rule out any: When you start exploring, you might be surprised to find out what works for you and your life.

Self-Brand Strategy 1: Be the First

Everyone knows being first is an advantage. The first mover generally ends up the leader in the category; because it's the leader, everyone believes it to be the best in its category, and so it is often the one we keep in mind.

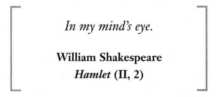

In my mind's eye.

William Shakespeare
Hamlet **(II, 2)**

Being first is a formidable advantage. Michael Dell was the first direct seller of personal computers and currently dominates that business. Jeff Bezos created the first online retail book marketplace, and it is still number one. The list goes on and on.

You're probably thinking, "These are business giants, and this kind of accomplishment would be impossible for a mere mortal like me. How can I be number one in anything?"

You don't have to be brilliant to create a first. New categories are popping up all the time, as you'll see once you start looking. You just need the proper mind-set. Often, you can slice a category to create a new subcategory, or niche, and be first in that. Or you can think of it in Darwinian terms as *divergence*, which is how Al Ries and Laura Ries describe forming new brand categories in their book *The Origin of Brands*.

The *be the first strategy* is very successful for entrepreneurs, but executives can use it, too. Enterprising employees or intrapreneurs often create new market niches—whether it is a new type of product, service, or customer niche. These firsts may end up being enormously profitable for the company and for the employee's self-brand. And there are lots of different ways to slice up a category and create a new area to be first in, as you will see in the next brainstormer.

If you can't think of anything, read *The Origin of Brands* and try the exercise again. If you still come up blank, think about the question again before going to sleep, and you'll have answers in the morning.

<< BRAINSTORMER >>

Uncovering New Firsts

Look at your business or what you do as something that can be sliced in various ways to make new categories or subcategories.

What new categories or subcategories can you create?

Self-Brand Strategy 2: Be the Leader

There are many ways of creating a *leader strategy*. You could be the leader of your department, your company, or your favorite charity. Or you might be the leader in sales at your company or the leader in sales in a segment of the market.

Many professionals have leadership claims and feel they are acting like leaders, yet they are not perceived as leaders. To be *perceived* as a leader, you must *lead with ideas* and *lead by example*.

> *Suit the action to the word, the word to the action.*
>
> **William Shakespeare**
> *Hamlet* **(III, 2)**

As a leader, you have to be able to articulate ideas that are worthy of being remembered, and you must be able to inspire others. Ideally, you want your employees or target audience to think you own a word or an idea so that they know what your battle cry is. Most important, you must underscore your ideas with actions, preferably bold actions that demonstrate what you stand for.

Emily had recently been promoted to head a department at her company. Her first task was to rally her team under her leadership.

In order to articulate a department mission, Emily created the mantra "full engagement." She wanted to introduce a new sense of engagement—a passion for excellence, a focus on clients and innovation.

Emily asked each of her managers for a five-page memo outlining key initiatives, including what the company could do to get employees more engaged with clients and with the business itself. She then implemented the best suggestions.

Her group's focus on full engagement landed more business and created a dynamic spirit at the company. It also positioned Emily as a leader.

‹‹ BRAINSTORMER ››

Becoming a Leader

Pick up **Winning,** by Jack Welch with Suzy Welch. It's a primer on business leadership and includes numerous examples of the mind-set and behaviors of business leaders.

What can you do to establish yourself as a leader?

Self-Brand Strategy 3: Take the Anti-Leader Position

As much as leaders are part of the mythology of our country, so are underdogs. We have a soft spot for the rebel, the lone defier of convention who doesn't follow the established path.

> *Oh, what dare men do!*
>
> **William Shakespeare**
> *Much Ado About Nothing* **(IV, 1)**

Volkswagen put the *anti-leader strategy* on the map when it introduced the Beetle to the United States in the late 1960s. The brand was positioned as the antidote to the big-car habit, with now-classic advertising headlines like "Think Small" and "Lemon."

Also, for every Microsoft, there is an Apple, a brand that symbolizes the opposite of the dominant leader to its customers. An especially powerful tactic of the anti-leader position strategy is casting the entrenched leader as the evil empire. Microsoft's competitors have touched that nerve with technology consumers.

In the self-brand category, Michael Moore is a classic example. His movies and books tweak the establishment, whether it's the automobile industry (*Roger and Me*), the National Rifle Association and the gun lobby (*Bowling for Columbine*), or President George W. Bush and the war in Iraq (*Fahrenheit 9/11*).

The anti-leader position could be risky, particularly if you work in a corporation (although many do have a few maverick employees). It is a self-brand strategy adopted mainly by people who are either confident in their positions or have nothing to lose.

However, taking the anti-leader position may be a great strategy for entrepreneurs. You build your company's point of difference as the antidote to the leader by positioning the leader's strengths as weaknesses, as the chart below shows. You and your company symbolize everything the leader is not.

LEADER	VS. ANTI-LEADER POSITION
Big	Small and nimble
Slow	Fast and responsive
Out of touch	Cutting-edge
Bureaucratic	Entrepreneurial
Dull	Creative and alive
Impersonal	Personal
Inflexible	Flexible
One size fits all	Custom
Expensive	Good value
Unresponsive	Responsive

‹‹ BRAINSTORMER ››

Taking the Opposites Test

Identify the leaders in your company, industry, or selected arena.

Outline what they stand for, their image, and the attributes or adjectives that are associated with them.

For each leader, determine the **opposite** position, image, or attributes.

The anti-leader position is a brand strategy that generally offers a great PR platform for you and your business. Mavericks provide good ink for the media. (Think Richard Branson and Virgin.)

So, if you like to go against the grain, the anti-leader position may be for you.

The strategy is simplicity itself. Whatever the leader in your industry or line of work is doing, think of doing the opposite (within reason). Brainstorm it. You could find a market that is looking for someone just like you.

Self-Brand Strategy 4: Own an Attribute

The most common positioning strategy for brands is to *own an attribute*. Mercedes-Benz's brand strategy is built around prestige, BMW's is driving performance, Subaru's is ruggedness, and Volvo's is safety.

> *Assume a virtue if you have it not.*
>
> **William Shakespeare**
> *Hamlet* **(III, 4)**

For this strategy to work best, you should select the brand attribute that is credible for *you* to own and gives you maximum opportunity in your category.

For example, when Pampers first developed the disposable diaper in the early 1960s, sales were poor. The marketing was positioned around convenience, a brand attribute that had a clear-cut benefit for busy moms. Moms didn't have to clean and disinfect the diapers themselves or use an expensive diaper service. Convenience was especially beneficial for moms on the go with their babies. They didn't have to carry stinky cloth diapers around with them until they got home. But that attribute positioning didn't resonate with mothers. They felt guilty. Cloth diapers were best for babies, while paper diapers were best for moms. So moms voted with their hearts, and sales were poor.

Then Pampers changed its brand positioning to "better absorbency," which was a benefit for babies. Mothers could buy the diapers and feel that they were doing what was best for their babies, not best for them. Sales took off, and cloth diapers and diaper services went the way of the buggy whip.

Snag the Best Attribute Available

Every category is associated with attributes that are important to customers and prospects. And you can slice your industry, profession, or job category to find the best fit for the attribute you want to own and the category in which you want to do it. This is true regardless of your industry, whether it's financial services, manufacturing, marketing, law, medicine, academia, or what have you.

Your job as a self-brander is to stake your claim to the attribute that is best for you and is not owned by a competitor in the arena where you will have the most impact.

One client, Benjamin, had just been promoted to president of his company. The good news: it was a great job. The bad news: it was a difficult job. Sales revenue was down, and his industry was in a serious slump. Benjamin's first task was to rally the troops and unify the company, particularly the division heads, most of whom were strong personalities with a tight grip on their fiefdoms.

We built Benjamin's personal-brand strategy around the attribute of "accountability." It was an important attribute, one that many colleagues and employees associated with him because of his track record. Other executives might have great creative skills or people skills, as Benjamin did, but none matched his sense of accountability and follow-through.

‹‹ BRAINSTORMER ››

Who Owns the Important Attributes

If you described your brand with one adjective or attribute that expresses your personal truth, it would be _____.

What attributes or characteristics are important in your line of work or in your business?

What attributes are already owned by competitors, either other people or other companies?

What's available for you?

Accountability was an important attribute for the company at this juncture. In Benjamin's estimation, the company's problem was not a lack of innovative ideas but the inability to follow through internally (by getting all the various departments to work together) and with clients (by focusing on being a real business partner, not simply on closing).

Benjamin wanted to lead by example in terms of accountability with colleagues and clients, and he also took positive action to embed the attribute in the company culture. One of the first things he did was broadcast his management philosophy to all the employees: His rallying cry was "Everyone's accountable, everywhere, all the time."

Self-Brand Strategy 5: Use a Magic Ingredient or Invent a New Process

Having a magic ingredient or creating a new process is one of the oldest brand strategies, dating back to the origins of branding—the patent medicines of the 18th and 19th centuries.

The strategy works well for consultants, doctors, researchers, scientists, and other professionals if value added comes from what they use or how they go about their work.

> *A dish fit for the gods.*
>
> **William Shakespeare**
> *Julius Caesar* **(II, 1)**

The occupation of chef tended to be rather mundane. Chefs were closer to working stiffs than sought-after celebrities. That is, until some chefs adopted the *magic ingredient strategy*, and the celebrity chef was born. (Think of Julia Child, James Beard, Wolfgang Puck, Mario Batali, and "Naked Chef" Jamie Oliver, for example.) Today, in top restaurants, the chef is often more of a marquee attraction than the well-known customers are.

Any innovative executive or professional can use the *new process strategy* by reexamining a process or procedure and developing a new approach with his or her name tag on it.

<‹ BRAINSTORMER ›>

Searching for a New Mousetrap

Look carefully at your company, industry, school, or profession. Also look at your target audience and current products or services. Then consider the following questions.

What are the shortcomings in the current way things are done and what frustrations do they cause?

What do customers complain about?

Is there a new component or process that could solve the problem?

What could customers really like to have that they don't get now?

Self-Brand Strategy 6: Be the Expert

Being a jack-of-all-trades is not a smart strategy; it is smart to be an expert in one area.

Focus is powerful. The narrower the focus, the more powerful the brand. This is an era in which specialists thrive and generalists do not.

In executing the *expert strategy*, it helps to be able to interpret something in a new way. One solution is to choose an area that is not already crowded with experts so that you can be dominant. Or you could choose an area where the current experts are not doing a good job of communicating. Look where there is a need for better information and interpretation or a fresh point of view.

Our space

> *Ignorance is the curse of god,*
> *Knowledge the way.*
>
> **William Shakespeare**
> *Henry VI* **(IV, 7)**

The expert strategy propelled Barbara Corcoran into the stratosphere in the New York City real estate brokerage community. With fewer than a dozen real estate sales to her name, Barbara Corcoran created a marketplace report called *The Corcoran Report* and sent it to all the newspapers.

Formerly a nobody, Corcoran became *the* real estate expert in New York City when the first issue of her report landed on the front page of the Sunday *New York Times* real estate section.

Corcoran recounts this and other tales of how she outsmarted the ladies in mink (the establishment brokers) and even Donald Trump in her book *Use What You've Got, and Other Business Lessons I Heard from My Mom.* (Corcoran rebranded the paperback edition of the book with a sexier title, *If You Don't Have Big Breasts, Put Ribbons in Your Pigtails.* Her publisher had talked her out of using this title for the original hardcover edition.)

So consider carving out a niche where you can be the expert. Remember, the media is always looking for a new face, someone who will interpret something. The makeover craze has spawned new experts on the media stage—hairdressers, image consultants, and stylists. The popularity of home and garden improvement has created a strong market for expert renovators, carpenters, and gardeners.

The expert strategy is perfectly suited to tactics like newsletters, workshops, media interviews, and bylined columns. The book route is another smart way to go. If you have written a book, you are instantly an expert. And your book tour is a great way to promote your expertise and your business.

‹‹ BRAINSTORMER ››

Becoming the Expert

In what subject are you particularly knowledgeable?

New Strategy

Who are the authorities on the subject?

How does your point of view differ from those of other experts?

What can you do to become more of an authority? To be perceived as the authority? (For example, you could convince your company to fund a research study, or you could write an article on the topic.)

Published
Power Broker
+ Auk

Self-Brand Strategy 7: Be Preferred

You can build your brand strategy around your users: the target market that prefers your services.

A surefire winner is to be the preferred choice of an elite group. Examples are the financial consultant who manages high-society money, the investment banker whose Rolodex is filled with the names of CEOs, the plastic surgeon who works on celebrity faces. To protect their clients' privacy, names often aren't publicized but are leaked to the press or passed along by word of mouth. Stealth PR like this further enhances preferences among the cognoscenti.

> *Sell when you can.*
> *You are not for all markets.*
>
> **William Shakespeare**
> *As You Like It* (III, 5)

In developing the *preferred strategy* for yourself, the hardest part is getting the first high-profile client. Once you have done this, that client is a powerful lure for others.

everyone awesome client Base

But the preference strategy doesn't have to be based on celebrities or high-profile people. In chapter 2, we introduced Alexandra, who had a generic executive coaching business that began to flourish when she narrowed her focus to a particular client group: difficult people and the people who work for them. By focusing on the subgroup that she enjoyed working with and with whom she was most successful, Alexandra expanded her business. She also appeared on cable TV talk shows to comment on coping strategies and the like.

The following brainstormer will help you pinpoint your key target audience.

‹‹ BRAINSTORMER ››

Who Prefers You?

Have you had consistent success with a specific group? Could that group become the focus of your self-brand identity? Name or describe the group.

Tough one - open minded, unbiased people Geographic, Albany

non-profit?

Self-Brand Strategy 8: Set a High Price

Setting a high price on your services is a good strategy for standing out and garnering business. For many people, high price equates with superiority. It seems obvious that the $400-an-hour consultant *must* be better than the $100-an-hour consultant (or lawyer or doctor or creative director). How else could they charge that much? And the CEO who is paid $20 million must be better than the one who is paid a mere $1 million.

> *He is well paid that is well satisfied.*
>
> **William Shakespeare**
> *The Merchant of Venice* (IV, 1)

Of course, high price is a very elitist standard. It appeals to the desire for prestige, and being able to afford high prices encourages a feeling of superiority. This elite status might be manifested by a pricey new sports car, a mansion, or an expensive business adviser.

Anyone who uses this strategy must be able to demonstrate in some way that he or she is worth it. In some cases, having a high profile is enough for implementing this strategy.

Many high-priced consultants, lobbyists, and bankers come from prestigious government positions that enable them to cash in when they enter the private sector.

The *high price strategy* is a tough act to pull off. You've got to have the confidence to push away some desirable opportunities if the price isn't right. You've also got to convey the impression that you are "hard to get." For example, you may only accept new clients through high-level referrals, or maybe appointments have to be made months in advance. It's not for everyone; but that's the basis of this strategy.

Self-Brand Strategy 9: Use Your Special Heritage

If your last name is Bush, Kennedy, or Rockefeller, you have not only the money but a special heritage that is brand heaven in terms of the leverage it gives you. Offspring with a family-name brand are often able to start out at third base while the rest of us have to begin at home plate.

‹‹ BRAINSTORMER ››

Pricing Power

Explore these possibilities for justifying a high price strategy.

Do you have a superior track record, special accomplishments, or a special background that would justify a high price?

Do you have the self-confidence to pull it off?

Even if your name doesn't appear in the social register, you could leverage the *special heritage strategy* through national origin, a prestigious school, apprenticeship in a well-regarded training program, or a stint at a well-known company.

BIBA

> *A good wit makes use of anything.*
>
> **William Shakespeare**
> *Henry IV, Part 2* (I, 2)

For example, earlier in this chapter, you met Anthony. He didn't have a famous family heritage, but he did have his Indian heritage, his grandfather's business reputation, and a void in the market.

I had no family heritage connections, but I took advantage of my educational heritage when I was unable to obtain permission to view paintings in private collections for my Ph.D. dissertation in Japanese art. I had a business card printed up in English and in Japanese listing my educational credentials: Ph.D. student, Harvard University; foreign exchange student, Tokyo University; recipient, Japanese Ministry of Education Fellowship. Was it a little over the top? In America, yes; in Japan, no. Did it work? You bet.

In addition to school pedigree, there is company heritage. Employment with some companies is like having a stamp of approval associated with your name. On Wall Street, it's Goldman Sachs. In consulting, it's McKinsey. In packaged goods, it's Procter & Gamble.

Top company brands attract the best and the brightest. (At least, that's the perception.) So people will assume that you are, too. Top company brands put their new hires through a rigorous training program and keep them on the cutting edge of best practices. So people will think you know your stuff. Company heritage gives you a formidable advantage. Think of all the Fortune 100 CEOs with a General Electric heritage.

A lot of people who achieve fame in one career are able to leverage their heritage to achieve success in a new endeavor. For example, many prominent politicians or government officials go on to head up companies. Or prominent people in business or entertainment go into politics. (Think Michael Bloomberg in New York City and Arnold Schwarzenegger in California.)

<< BRAINSTORMER >>

Exploring Your Heritage

What connections could you leverage from your family, schools, training programs, country of origin, awards or distinctions, political office, or company heritage?

Sonny Bono told the story of how he knew his entertainment career was over when he mispronounced a name on *Fantasy Island*. Of course, he felt like a has-been when the other guests started ridiculing him on air. In that moment, Sonny decided that this was it for show business. He went on to open a restaurant and enter politics, leveraging his celebrity heritage to rebrand himself successfully.

Being part of an elite group or training program also taps into the heritage strategy. Look at Teach for America, which attracts the best and the brightest college graduates to teach at some of the most challenging schools in the United States. It's a badge of distinction often used as a way to contribute to society and gain real-world experience before applying to a prestigious graduate school.

Self-Brand Strategy 10: Own a Cause

For many people, doing something meaningful and significant is much more important than achieving the standard definition of success. Olivia started a women's initiative in her company, promoting leadership development, mentoring, and a more women-friendly culture throughout the company.

> *To business that we love*
> *we rise betime and to't with delight.*
>
> **William Shakespeare**
> ***Antony and Cleopatra* (IV, 4)**

Olivia is passionate about furthering women in her company, but championing the cause has been great for her career as well. She is highly visible in the company and has developed a great network with all the dynamic women who work there. Olivia's cause has also been a conduit for raising her profile with senior management, which has helped her immensely in achieving in her own career ambitions.

Being synonymous with a cause or creating a new cause has propelled many people onto a bigger stage. Think of Martin Luther King Jr. and the civil rights movement or Gloria Steinem and women's liberation. In his remarkable quest to alleviate Third World debt and poverty, Bono

<< BRAINSTORMER >>

Finding Your Cause

Is there a cause or issue that you are passionate about? Is there a cause that you would like to create and champion?

has taken his rock star power to the United Nations, the G-8 summit, the World Economic Forum at Davos, and the White House (just to highlight a few of his venues).

Through his work for Habitat for Humanity, Jimmy Carter rebuilt his image. He went from a former president who ranked low in the court of public opinion to a leader who was admired for his hands-on work helping the poor and brokering peace deals around the world. His humanitarian and peace initiatives earned him the ultimate accolade for a self-brand with strong humanitarian goals, the Nobel Peace Prize. And George H. W. Bush and Bill Clinton serve as a highly effective disaster relief duo raising money for natural catastrophes like the Asian tsunami and Hurricane Katrina.

GET GREAT RESULTS WITH A STRATEGY

In this chapter, you have explored 10 self-brand strategies:

1. Be the first
2. Be the leader
3. Take the anti-leader position
4. Own an attribute
5. Use a magic ingredient or invent a new process
6. Be the expert

7. Be preferred

8. Set a high price tag

9. Use your special heritage

10. Own a cause

Try each on for size to see if it fits. You might be surprised to see which one has potential for you.

To be fully free to develop your self-brand strategy, you must find the confidence to let go. You have to let go of what worked in the past. Let go of your assumptions of what would work in the future. Let go of feeling powerless and small. Often, the strategy you reject the quickest is the very one that has enormous promise for your career success.

A great way to conduct your strategy exploration is to create the kind of war room used by ad agencies and marketing boutiques. You might find it easier to jump-start the process and pluck the winners from the losers if you can see the different strategies you are considering hanging on the walls.

Write a strategy for yourself based on the format in the next brainstormer.

‹‹ BRAINSTORMER ››

Creating a Self-Brand Strategy

Choose 1 out of the 10 self-brand strategies and then think of proof points, or reasons why your target audience would believe this brand is true of you.

My brand is

because

On a basic level, your self-brand strategy statement represents a promise. It's a promise of what your brand has to offer its target audience. The support points are the reasons to believe that promise, why *you*—and not others—can deliver on that promise.

Put your various brand strategies up on a wall. Then, one by one, take down the weaker contenders. The one that's left will be your winner—your self-brand strategy.

<< IN A NUTSHELL >>

The fourth secret of self-brands:

Develop a strategy that gives you a winnable position,

a strategy that gives people a reason for choosing you

and not your competitor.

USE THE PRINCIPLES OF VISUAL IDENTITY TO CREATE A POWERFUL SELF-BRAND PACKAGE

> *Apparel oft proclaims the man.*
>
> **William Shakespeare**
> *Hamlet* **(I, 3)**

It may seem superficial. It may be unfair. We may not like it. After all, why should you by judged by your looks?

Self-presentation—your visual identity—is important because of the *link* people make between what something looks like on the outside and what is on the inside. This attitude has a long history. The ancient Greeks and Romans felt that beauty of the body was synonymous with beauty of the spirit.

We do this even today despite all the familiar admonitions, such as "Beauty is only skin deep" or "Don't judge a book by its cover." The fact is, looks have a profound influence on our judgment of a brand or a person.

Good looks also have what social scientists call the *halo effect.* Because something is attractive, we assign many other positive attributes to it that have nothing to do with looks.

PACKAGE YOURSELF

That's why brand managers are masters of visual identity. The way something looks is often the point of first (and lasting) impact for a brand.

Product design and packaging are quick ways of communicating the brand message. They make something more interesting and memorable. They may even clinch the sale.

Although they are wordless, a brand's packaging and design speak to us in color, shape, and material. Brands speak through imagery and symbols in logos, packaging, and advertising.

Visuals speak a universal language.

It's the same with people. Everything communicates visually—from your shoes to the watch you wear, your hairstyle to your smile (or frown), your home address to the car you drive. All these things say something about you and contribute to the perceptions people form about you.

Visual identity tells us whether a brand is expensive or cheap, fun or serious, unusual or commonplace. A brand's visual presentation sells to us as adeptly as any salesperson does, sometimes even more so.

Packaging and design help differentiate a brand among all the other brands vying for attention in the marketplace. And, like art, great design slows us down to admire and savor it and want the brand for our very own.

Visual identity is such a powerful competitive tool today that even manufacturers and retailers of low-priced brands are turning to well-known artists, architects, designers, and celebrities to spiff up their products. Target has Isaac Mizrahi and Michael Graves on its roster. Kmart has Martha Stewart leading the pack. Wal-Mart has Mary-Kate and Ashley Olsen. H&M used Karl Lagerfeld, and Stella McCartney, daughter of Beatle Paul McCartney, has signed on to design clothes for the retail chain. It's now chic for well-known designers and celebrities to maintain a low-priced line.

SEIZE THE FIRST TWO SECONDS

We are pegged in a matter of seconds: good—bad, hire—don't hire, hip—stodgy, successful—loser, like—dislike.

It all happens in the first few seconds. We've all been there. The job candidate is barely in the door and is already sized up. Maybe we've even eliminated that person as a contender.

It's based on snap visual impressions: how people enter the room, how they look, their clothes, how they carry themselves, their facial expressions and body language. We make up our minds about who they are and what they are like (even what they are worth), and they haven't said a word.

In *Blink*, Malcolm Gladwell talks about these snap judgments, which social scientists call "thin slicing." The interesting thing is that the instantaneous thin slice is usually the same as the impression we have after longer exposure.

Gladwell cites the research of the Tufts professor Nalini Ambady as proof. Ambady has focused her research on the snap judgments people make based on nonverbal clues such as gender, appearance, personality, and relationships. It took only *two* seconds for people to develop a strong first impression.

MAKE A GOOD FIRST IMPRESSION

For most of us, the same is true. Our hasty first impression will be indelible.

First impressions are so powerful in business that one client, Susan, has built a successful business as a fashion coach, writer, and speaker around the importance of a first impression not only in establishing *who* you are but also in selling how *good* you are.

We're all guilty of snap judgments based on looks. We're programmed to respond better to good-looking people. When shown pictures of people they view as "attractive" compared to those they label "unattractive," most people are biased toward attractive people.

Attractive people have the advantage of the halo effect. People with good looks are consistently deemed smarter, more likeable, talented, successful, and better in so many ways.

The good news is that ideas of "appealing," "attractive," and "successful" have expanded tremendously today as more people with unconventional looks succeed in spite of, or because of, unusual features. Different looks can be a powerful branding device, particularly if they are packaged as "interesting."

ACCENTUATE THE DIFFERENCE

This strategy does not work in every industry, but different looks not only get you noticed but may be smart brand positioning. Today, we face a sea of choices dominated by sameness in so many areas that an unusual-looking brand is very fetching.

Originally, Absolut's ad agency considered a heritage strategy for the Swedish brand's launch in the United States. Then, the creative team opted for a campaign based on the brand's distinctively shaped bottle. The ad campaign won tons of creative awards, and Absolut entered the big time. The brand went from a small contender, selling 12,000 cases a year in 1980, to the market leader in imported vodka, selling 2.7 million cases a decade later.

Many spirits and beverage manufacturers use a bottle with an unusual shape as part of their brand identity. For many customers and prospects, the shape alone is sufficient to identify the brand. Coca-Cola brought back its curvy bottle after having abandoned it for many years. The bottle was originally designed so that its shape could be recognized by touch in a dark refrigerator in the middle of the night. New beverages such as POM Wonderful pomegranate juice give the hourglass bottle shape an important role in advertising and branding.

Entertainment and sports celebrities often adopt an unusual look so they will stand out. Michael Jackson is probably the poster child for using this strategy to drive his personal brand, and there are lots of less extreme but equally successful examples: Barbra Streisand, Andy Warhol, Diana Vreeland, Alfred Hitchcock, and Arnold Schwarzenegger all dramatized their unusual looks, features, or shape.

HARNESS THE MAGIC IN YOU

Unlike new products, none of us can create a self-brand from scratch. We have to build off of who we are and what we look like. This is true whether your visual identity is lacking or strong. But everything has potential. Many brands languish until someone comes along with the smarts and creativity to revive the brand image and maximize its assets. Look at the renaissance at Apple Computer where a strong visual identity helped revive the brand.

So to start, you have to focus on yourself. Don't begin by copying the visual identities of people you admire. It is good to be inspired, but you'll never be remembered if you are a clone of someone else. Your visual identity should come out of your personality and preferences.

A good way to start developing your visual identity is by doing a personal visual inventory. What is your best feature? Worst feature? Explore what's different about you (height, shape, hair, features, expressions). What should you emphasize? Or de-emphasize?

WHAT IS YOUR VISUAL IDENTITY SAYING?

Visual identity is about visually communicating the message you want to convey. And when it really clicks, visual identity and message are one.

Look at your wardrobe and how you put yourself together. What do you want your entire package to say about you? Is it consistent with your self-brand strategy? Is there a signature feature or trademark accessory you could use to heighten your visual identity?

These are all questions you will want to deal with if you intend to maximize your visual identity. If you don't communicate the right message, or send out confusing messages, or fade into the wallpaper, you are undercutting your effectiveness. As one way of identifying the messages their brands trigger, brand managers conduct visual association tests in focus groups. The brainstormer on the following page outlines an example of this kind of test.

CREATE VISUAL EXCITEMENT

An intriguing visual identity greatly accelerates the value of your brand in any kind of business. Sofia Coppola first came into the public spotlight, and was panned, in her father's movie, *The Godfather, Part III*. When she changed her brand category from actor to independent director, her self-brand took off. And she capitalized on her accomplishments with a distinctive, cool visual style, becoming the designer Marc Jacobs's muse.

<< BRAINSTORMER >>

The Visual Association Test

Try doing this test yourself. Then ask a few friends to participate so that you can find out what visual associations they make with you. The purpose is not to copy but to get creative inspiration for your brand identity.

If you were a famous person, who would it be?

Describe that person's visual identity: look, style, clothing, accessories, etc.

Why is that person right for you? Probe the association. How can this person inspire your visual identity?

If you were a car, what type of car would it be?

Describe the car in as much detail as possible. Why does it symbolize you?

If you were an animal what would it be? Why?

The great fashion sense and hip image of tennis players like Venus Williams, Serena Williams, and Andre Agassi probably didn't help them win more games. But they did help these athletes build powerful brand identities that translated into more bucks in endorsement contracts.

Inspiration for a distinct visual identity could come from anywhere. In the conservative financial services industry, Tom Gardner and David Gardner stole inspiration from the medieval fool when they launched their highly successful personal investing company Motley Fool. They even donned the motley hats of the medieval fool in media appearances in order to build awareness and underscore their untraditional thinking. Granted, most of us would feel silly in this persona, but it was smart personal branding in a crowded category.

Rodale Press went against the grain in developing a visual identity for the South Beach Diet that was different from the serious, almost textbook-like appearance common to the diet-book genre. Instead, Rodale's metallic blue book jacket was inspired by South Beach's trademark Art Deco palette.

LET YOUR CLOTHES TALK

Strong visual identities are a quick read. And clothes are one of the quickest ways to communicate a message about who you are. Clothes often offer more insight than your curriculum vitae.

> *Sure this robe of mine does change my disposition.*
>
> **William Shakespeare**
> *The Winter's Tale* **(IV, 4)**

Clothes communicate what you do for a living and whether you are rich or poor, young or old, hip or square, professional or blue collar. They often express whether you are looking for a mate or a new job or just don't give a damn.

Clothes are such a strong branding device that for centuries there were laws in many regions of the world about who could wear what. Only certain classes could wear certain colors, fabrics, and clothing styles.

Think of the drill you put yourself through for an important meeting or job interview. "What shall I wear?" goes racing through your brain as you tear through your closet. What you choose can help or hinder you in the meeting.

These days there is no simple "dress for success" formula. Today, you have more latitude in using clothes to communicate your personal brand message.

The suit is the package for most executives. Suits are practically a uniform for men, although the fabric and fit can be distinguishing features.

> **Clothes won't make a big difference in how well you do your job, yet they will have a significant effect on how you are perceived on the job.**

Women have more freedom to brand a personal identity with their corporate uniform. If your clothes could talk, what would they say about you? Is there a consistent message? What do you want your clothes to say about you? Which pieces of clothing should you eliminate? Which pieces of clothing should you build on? Choose your clothes and personal style to communicate what you want to say about yourself. Clothes are a visual symbol of who you are.

SEND VISUAL CLUES

Remember the gray poncho Martha Stewart wore when she was released from prison? It became the indelible image of Martha Stewart leaving prison. The poncho was a handmade gift from a fellow inmate, and Martha wore it for her dramatic exit from prison and on her first day back at the office.

The poncho was a brilliant branding device because it enabled Stewart to convey the right messages for rebranding herself. Her new image said,

> Martha is back on top of her game

> Martha made lemonade out of lemons

> Martha bonded with her fellow prisoners

> Martha can pluck style out of anywhere

> Martha is stronger because of this experience

With her prison poncho, Stewart took control of her brand message. Remember how she looked in the months leading up to her conviction? In a word, guilty. She was hiding from the press, often caught looking unglamorous and shielding her face. The poncho put her self-brand back on track.

LOOK THE PART TO GET THE PART

Looking good is the price of admission in some careers. In most companies, if your goal is the corner office, you have to look successful.

Many times, just looking the part gets you at least halfway there. Looking the part often works like a self-fulfilling prophecy. What you build in other people's minds through images has a way of coming true.

From the crown of his head to the sole of his foot.

William Shakespeare
Much Ado about Nothing **(III, 2)**

When French president François Mitterand first met Ronald Reagan, he remarked, "Il a vraiment la notion de l'etat" (He really has a sense of the state about him). The *role*—in the case of the president, symbolizing the head of state—is an important part of the *job* of being president. We want people to satisfy a visual image of a key role, particularly the important ones. It is hard to become president of the United States if you don't *seem* presidential.

Not looking the part may be a career buster for people at all levels, as Lauren found out. Without realizing it, she had been branded—and in a way that hurt her career ambitions.

Lauren was a talented account executive at an advertising agency in New York City. She had an image problem and didn't know it. Her drive and hard work had gotten her to the mid-level as an account supervisor, but she was stuck there, and she didn't know why.

Lauren had a senior-level workload but not the title, money, and perks that go with it. The situation with her boss had even started to get uncomfortable. He excluded her from new business presentations, although she worked on them behind the scenes, because he didn't feel she was ready. She was clearly good enough to do the work but not good enough to be onstage.

Lauren was from a working-class family in New Jersey. She was a self-made person, but she had never completely left her working-class roots behind. She could create a successful brand-image campaign at the agency, but she had not transferred that skill to her own image.

TUNE INTO THE COMPANY UNIFORM

It may seem superficial, but image reigns in many professions, such as Lauren's.

Each industry and individual company has a culture and a visual identity that can be analyzed. And while most of the rules are hidden and unspoken, they are there just the same.

You need to decode the unspoken dress codes. Look around at work. What is the dress style of your company? On the executive floor? How do these styles dovetail with your style?

In *Who Says Elephants Can't Dance?* Louis Gerstner recounts a telling tale about the IBM company uniform. On his first day as CEO, Gerstner was in a meeting with his key executives, wearing his standard suit and blue shirt. Every male executive was wearing a white shirt, which was IBM's "uniform" at the time. The next day, all the men showed up at the office in blue shirts. And Gerstner was wearing a white shirt!

As the Bard said, "we have our exits and entrances and in our time play many parts." But in Lauren's case, she was doing all the work backstage and had no chance to play a part. In business, meetings are the primary stage on which you perform, and if you are left out of the important meetings, you're in big trouble.

Lauren was doing casual Mondays, Tuesdays, Wednesdays, Thursdays, and Fridays. Low-rise jeans and a hip shirt might be okay every day in the creative department, but not on the account management floor, where trendy was the style and Friday was for dressy casual. The "casualization" of American business has gone overboard, and many companies are reverting to dress codes or more formal attire in an attempt to rein in the flip-flops and denim.

TAKE THE MAKEOVER PLUNGE

It was not a fun message to give to a client, nor was it well received at first. Gradually, however, Lauren came around and embraced a makeover and a visual identity that suited her, the advertising business, and her agency.

It wasn't about spending a lot of money. Though she needed to jazz things up a bit for the agency biz and have some of what the French call *bon chic, bon genre* (good style, good attitude), it was about looking good in order to promote confidence in what she was saying.

It was about creating a visual identity that communicated "powerful, dynamic woman on the move," which was what she had wanted to stand for all along. It was about self-actualization, becoming more herself, without letting irrelevant things hold her back.

The better Lauren became at looking and acting the part, the more confident she felt about her business abilities, and the more high-profile assignments she got at the agency.

Then, at some point, no one even remembered the dowdy Lauren except the ones who were jealous of her career rise. But that didn't affect her one bit.

Lauren even framed a picture of the modest, white frame house where she had grown up in New Jersey and displayed it prominently on one of the walls in her office. She was proud of her origins. She had made it through her own hard work and talent. But she wasn't holding herself back with a poor visual identity anymore.

DON'T LOOK PERFECT

Perfection is not as appealing as a more approachable look. I have worked with some people who had that problem. A perfect visual identity conveys "slick" or "unapproachable." Most people find perfection a barrier to likeability. And that, no doubt, is not what you want to achieve.

> **Perfect reads plastic. Overdone reads trying too hard.**

You always want to come across as real. If you decide to try for perfection, leave something imperfect, like a carefree hairstyle or a slightly worn briefcase, so that you appear accessible and likeable.

DON'T IGNORE YOUR HAIR

Hair is a terrific branding device. Think of Dolly Parton vs. Laura Bush. Don King vs. Dr. Phil. Like clothing, hair used to be a branding device in many parts of the world. Your hairstyle indicated your status in society or what you did for a living.

Donald Trump's hair has become as much a trademark of his visual identity as the trophy wife and oversize yacht. So, make fun of it or not, the hair stays because it is an important part of Trump's visual identity from a branding perspective.

Remember how Hillary Clinton kept changing her hairstyle when she was First Lady? Long. Then held back with a headband. Smoothed under at the ends. Flipped up. Then short. Clinton's hair became a media story for a while.

People were confused about who Hillary Clinton was because her hairstyle kept changing. Now that she has settled on a consistent (and attractive) style, she has removed a source of mixed messages that was undercutting her self-presentation and effectiveness.

HAVE A TRADEMARK

Developing a signature item as a trademark of your visual style is a good tactic for self-branding. You're creating a branding element that identifies you, like the logo on a product. Having that element will set you apart from the crowd. Chosen well, it will convey a brand message to others and even change the way you see yourself.

During his first trip to Europe, Benjamin Franklin followed the fashion on the Continent and wore a wig and a brocade jacket for state functions. Ever one to understand the value of self-promotion, Franklin bucked the trend and donned simple American broadcloth when he went to France later as the U.S. representative after the Revolution. He didn't wear a wig, and his loose gray hair under a marten fur cap became his signature look.

A trademark or signature accessory creates a visual identifier that works as a branding device.

Franklin's memorable image and coiffure only heightened his popularity and fame. He was hailed as a homespun philosopher and became the most famous person on the Continent.

‹‹ BRAINSTORMER ››

Creating Your Trademark

Here are some areas to explore in developing a signature item.

Is there a family heirloom or something personal from your family?

Do you have different taste in accessories (bow ties, suspenders, hats)?

Is there a feature or accessory you can emphasize (hairstyle, glasses)?

Is there a signature item that can brand your visual identity? Examples of signature items are endless. Jackie Kennedy had her pillbox hats and later oversize sunglasses. Margaret Thatcher had her purses. Larry King has his suspenders. George W. Bush has his cowboy boots. Katie Couric has her big smile. Barbra has her nose. Bono has his tinted wraparound sunglasses, as vivid a symbol for his brand as the golden arches are for McDonald's.

Your trademark could be an item you dispense with that everyone else wears. Katharine Hepburn eschewed skirts, and pants became her trademark in an era when most women didn't wear pants.

Sartorially, John F. Kennedy's trademark was his hatlessness. He did without a hat at a time when men wore hats everywhere, even to casual activities like baseball games.

Neil Steinberg, the author of the book *Hatless Jack*, writes, "Kennedy was lauded as this dashing, hatless guy whose adoring public followed his example and tossed away their hats."

DEVELOP YOUR VISUAL IDENTITY

Here are 10 guidelines to keep in mind as you develop your visual identity:

1. *Think of clothes as packaging:* Use clothes to enhance, not undercut, your brand message.

2. *Have a signature item:* Think of a trademark that people associate with you.

3. *Look different:* You don't want to look like everyone else. You want your own vibe.

4. *Look the part:* Fulfill expectations of your role and the style of the institution or target market to which you are appealing.

5. *Use hair as a branding device:* Think of Dolly Parton, Anna Wintour, and Donald Trump. Each has an unmistakable branded hairstyle.

6. *Make your look consistent:* Don't send mixed messages. Everything should tie together for a consistent visual identity at business, casual, and formal events.

7. *Have a signature color or palette:* Build your wardrobe and brand marketing around a related palette of colors for maximum effect.

8. *Have a strong presence:* How you stand and carry yourself gives you presence and helps make you memorable.

9. *Leverage your height, shape, or profile:* Build your visual identity off who you are.

10. *Stay relevant and fresh:* Let your brand evolve and stay up-to-date.

The whole point of visual identity for people is to maximize the non-verbal messages you are sending out about yourself.

Look at yourself as a package. Does your brand's message on the outside match your self-brand on the inside?

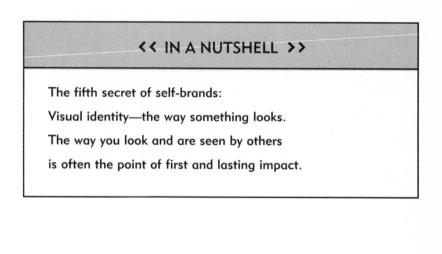

‹‹ IN A NUTSHELL ››

The fifth secret of self-brands:

Visual identity—the way something looks.

The way you look and are seen by others

is often the point of first and lasting impact.

TAP INTO THE POWER OF SYMBOLS, LOGOS, AND DESIGN TO IMPRINT YOUR BRAND IDENTITY

> *We are the stuff as dreams are made on.*
>
> **William Shakespeare**
> *The Tempest* **(IV, 1)**

Symbols and logos convey meaning and emotions nonverbally.

That's why symbols and logos have always been powerful in translating ideas, establishing identity, and building communities. Religious symbols like the cross and the Star of David are full of meaning. They express concepts and emotions that most of us would have difficulty expressing in words. Yet a religious symbol can do it in a flash.

The word "brand" comes from the burning stick or branding iron used to mark an animal (or a criminal) more than a thousand years ago. By the 19th century, the brand mark began to indicate ownership not just of animals but also of wine, beer, and other commodities.

There is another type of brand identifier or brand symbol that also goes back to ancient times. Visual symbols that represented a trade were placed outside a shop to identify it to passersby at a time when many people could not read. The striped pole outside a barber shop is a remnant of that tradition.

A flag could be regarded as the logo of a country. We salute and rally around the flag as a symbol of the country we hold dear. Coats of arms with family or clan symbols and colors may be looked on as personal or family logos.

You need to use visual imagery, too, if you want to build a strong self-brand. Symbols and design can improve how people respond to all of your business activities, from your presentations to informal meetings, from your Internet presence to your letterhead.

TAP INTO NONVERBAL MEANING

Life today is rampant with symbols and logos.

When a woman wears a pink ribbon, we know she is expressing a message about breast cancer. Another familiar symbol is a yellow ribbon tied around a tree, or a yellow ribbon decal on a car to symbolize waiting for the safe return of a loved one.

Once discreet, logos now loom large on clothes, especially handbags, belts, and shoes.

Events such as the Olympics and even big corporate events have logos. Logos like the Nike swoosh and the Coke wave are as familiar as the names of the products.

A logo is a special sort of symbol—a graphic that stands for something specific. It may seem like a small thing, but it can be very powerful in developing an identity and personality for a brand.

Logos become powerful when they are well conceived in terms of design, color, and inferred meaning. Then, they become symbols that have meaning and identifying power for broad groups of people.

> **A logo may look like a small thing, but it is big in importance to a brand.**

Milton Glaser designed the "I ❤ NY" logo using a symbol (a heart) instead of the word "love." It was so novel at the time of its creation in the mid-1970s and so widely understood that it took on a global life of its own. Now you can see the heart logo used with just about anything on T-shirts, mugs, and souvenirs around the world.

STRIVE FOR ICON VALUE

Imagery also imbues a brand with meaning. Look at the power of the images in fashion and beauty ads.

When an image is particularly potent among a wide group of people, it can become an icon, a symbol for an entire category or for an important idea that is universally understood. Marilyn Monroe is an icon of female beauty and sexuality. Elvis Presley, the king of rock 'n' roll, is an icon of youth and rebellion. Albert Einstein is an icon of intellectual brilliance. (We may not be able to explain it, but most of us know Einstein's equation for relativity, $E = mc^2$). Icons like Marilyn, Elvis, and Einstein are elastic in the sense that they appeal to many people and they can mean different things to different people. Each has a strong visual identity—a signature hairstyle, look, and way of dressing that is easily recognized and even impersonated. And each has an enduring presence and ongoing relevance—indeed, many icons are more powerful after death than they were in life.

> **BRAND ICON:** A symbol of mythic proportions that transcends time and place of origin.

A symbol or even a small detail of something larger may become universally recognized and understood like an icon if it conveys powerful emotional content to a broad group of people. Look at the famous detail of two fingers touching in Michelangelo's "The Creation of Adam" on the Sistine Chapel ceiling. The index finger of God reaches out to touch the index finger of Adam. This detail is such a potent image of man's creation that it has been called the masterpiece within the masterpiece. It has been reproduced so often and has evoked emotion in so many people that it has become almost a cliché.

This visual imagery was unique at the time Michelangelo conceived it. There is no correlation to text in the biblical book of Genesis. Nor were there any painting precedents. The sheer power of the image created a stir when people first viewed it in the 16th century, and it is still a powerful image that speaks to us today.

DESIGN TO DIFFERENTIATE

If you are an entrepreneur, you'll want to think about how a logo and a distinct look sets your brand apart. You'll want a logo and brand imagery that will help you stand out in the marketplace.

You want it to say something about your brand—to convey intellectual and emotional meaning about it. Design professionals are crucial in this area. If people don't tell you that you have a good logo and good branding, go back to the drawing board.

A logo may be a distinctive type treatment of a name. Type font and color treatment alone can create a powerful brand identity, like the purple and orange FedEx logo or the primary-colored Google logo.

Usually, a logo design is "carved in stone," and its usage is carefully controlled by the company's corporate identity people. Even though it's an all-type logo, the inventive people at Google break the consistency rule of corporate identity.

Google sometimes changes its logo and decorates it during important holidays or other events. For example, at Thanksgiving, the logo at the Website's home page incorporated a turkey and seasonal colors. It's an artful way to build an emotional connection between a brand and its customers through its tangible symbol, the logo.

USE A GRAPHIC SYMBOL

Many logos use a mark, or graphic element, along with the name. Sometimes the mark's identity becomes so familiar, like the Apple Computer apple, that the mark alone immediately identities the brand. No name is required.

For the SelfBrand logo, I wanted to capture the idea of self-branding. The graphic designer I worked with came up with this mark: a big red box with a black dot outside it and off-center.

You could look at the mark as an abstract representation of "I" for self or "I brand." Or you could look at it as meaning "thinking outside the box," which is core to my self-branding philosophy. Or the graphic could be a camera since branding is about identity.

We also played with the key idea of the transformative process of branding. So in the word part of the logo, we began with the word "self" in lowercase black letters. For the word "brand," however, we used all uppercase, with each letter in a different color, alluding to the transformative power of a branding makeover. (The full-color version of the logo can be seen at www.selfbrand.com.)

A logo or an appealing brand look plays a masterful role in locking in a company identity and attracting an audience. Here are the most important guidelines to live by in developing a logo:

> *Keep it simple:* A logo should be easy to understand and reproduce. It has to work in small venues, like a business card, and in medium-size venues such as Websites and brochures. It must also be able to step up to the plate and look good on large signage.

> *Be different:* Have a look that is distinct from those of your competitors. You don't want the design du jour.

> *Have a personality:* Your logo should convey nonverbal cues such as emotion and personality. Think of adjectives that communicate personality and style attributes as you develop the logo.

> *Be "stretchable":* A logo should be able to grow as the brand expands its footprint.

> *Convey meaning:* A logo should be an icon, not an illustration. It's better to suggest than to describe. Many abstract logos take on a powerful meaning, but if you have to explain your logo, go back to the drawing board.

TAP INTO DESIGN POWER

With all the competition companies face, design has become much more important. Computers and phones used to look dull. No longer.

Design is a way of adding sizzle to your brand. Even more, design provides your brand with strategic control over competitors. Look at how the design of the Guggenheim Museum put the industrial town of Bilbao, Spain, on the map.

Take the jeans category. Today, there are more than 1,000 jeans brands, according to a media report. For many people, telling the difference between jeans brands would be impossible without looking at the label. So jeans put their brand identities on the back right pockets. Any teenager or twentysomething can identify a designer or hip jeans brand by the stitched patterns or decoration on the back pocket. No brand logo is required.

Tap into the power of visual branding even if you're a corporate executive with no marketing role. Work with your company's graphic design department. You need to think in terms of visual packaging for important ideas or initiatives as well as for new products and services in your group.

Including a distinctive logo and presentation package in your overall pitch positions your project favorably even before you've said a word.

VISUALIZE YOUR STRATEGY

When you're developing your visual identity for business cards, presentations, your office, and the like, look at how successful branding experts have done it. For example, look at Tazo. Tazo did a great job of building a visual identity—logo, packaging, and product design—off its brand strategy.

Tazo was launched in the mid-1990s amid the reincarnation of coffee spearheaded by Starbucks. Tazo's founders were a small group of friends who wanted to launch the "reincarnation of tea." This was no mean feat in the United States, a country where tea was a distant second to coffee and often viewed as a beverage for people who are feeling sick.

In order to build high interest in the tea category, Tazo's founders came up with an intriguing concept for their new tea. They called it "Marco Polo meets Merlin."

Tazo created a special logo, packaging, and product design to bring the concept to life. They melded Far Eastern colors and style with magical and cryptic elements. They found an obscure type font for the logo that gives the name Tazo a coded quality, like an alchemic symbol. Of course, it wasn't all branding. The company developed tea flavors that matched the brand concept.

SAVOR THE SENSES

Tazo also capitalized on a new trend in branding, orchestrating a total sensory experience through sight, smell, and touch.

Each tea had a name, color, and design concept. Tazo gave customers a new experience in tea names—for example, Awake—not old stand-bys like English Breakfast. Each tea had an exotic smell.

The sensory experience was heightened through what Tazo called "the discoverability of the brand." Tazo layered packages within packages and messages within messages so that customers would repeatedly touch and experience the brand.

So how important was Tazo's visual identity to the brand's phenomenal success?

Many retailers were so enchanted with the Tazo packaging that they bought in quantity before they even sampled the new product. In relatively short order, Tazo was one of the top natural foods brands in the United States. Tazo's success got the attention of the megabrand Starbucks, which bought the tea company to augment its expansion in the beverage market.

OWN A SIGNATURE COLOR

A distinctive color makes for smart branding. Color creates a mood and identifies a brand personality for your company or individual product line. There's Cingular orange, UPS brown, American Express blue, and Coca-Cola red, just to name a few well-known brands and their signature colors. If you see someone with white earphones in their ears, you'll know they're using an iPod.

You can make color a dominant theme for your personal brand. Mark Twain bought a whole wardrobe of white suits after he noticed that he got a lot more attention walking down the street or at speaking appearances when he was wearing a white suit rather than a traditional dark suit. The white suit became part of his self-brand identity along with his novels, public speeches, and sound bites. A white suit plays a similar role for the writer Tom Wolfe today.

Using color could be as simple as having distinctively colored stationery. One business acquaintance has chosen this strategy, and when the blue envelope arrives, I immediately know the identity of the sender. Or you could have a signature color for your Website or blog.

PACKAGE YOUR BUSINESS DOCUMENTS

We are all familiar with brand packaging. Just the shape of an ice cream container tells us whether it is a premium brand or a discount brand.

Every business document or communication has a package too. Letters, handouts, pitch books, presentations, fax cover sheets—every document that you create on the job to sell or persuade or inform—can be made special if you view its presentation as packaging.

When you give a presentation or a talk, always prepare a handout that represents your brand footprint. You'll need a person with good computer skills and a sharp eye for layout and type fonts.

Make the business documents look beautiful or interesting or different. Choose a brand color for all your presentation folders. You could even develop a distinct layout for your presentation documents, with a colored rule around each page or a logo at the bottom. Or use even more creative approaches, depending on the business you are in. I used text messaging for the title of this book, *You Are a BRAND!*, to convey the idea that, like text messaging, branding has a quickness and immediacy. But I also wanted a boldly different graphic look for the book cover that would grab attention (and, hopefully, spark sales).

Think of ways to put your brand stamp on all your output, even your method of delivering a message. When you have an important message to send—a new business pitch or a job inquiry letter—put your packaging inside a different delivery package, such as FedEx, so that it will be branded as important to its recipient. Or have it hand delivered.

WOW THEM WITH YOUR BUSINESS CARD

Your business card does the heavy lifting in brand building. It is often the first or even the only thing people are presented with. And most people are likely to hold on to it.

Your business card has your name, job identity, and company identity all in a small, compact format. A business card should create excitement for your brand as well as identify it. The card should presell you and your company. To do that, you must convey the company's brand personality through the design, shape, type font, logo, graphics, and verbal messages such as the company slogan.

If you work for a company, your business card is no doubt corporate issue. You might want to create your own business card, one that sets the right image and tone, for personal use.

‹‹ BRAINSTORMER ››

The Business Card Test

Show your business card to five people.

What is the first response you get after handing out your card?

What is your message? Do people get the right message?

How would people describe your self-brand based on the business card?

How could you improve the card?

If you're an entrepreneur and people don't tell you that you have a great business card, go back to your designer. This is not an area to skimp on by selecting a template from an office supply store. It will look like a template design. It's worth hiring a graphic designer to help you develop a corporate identity for your business.

On the front of the card, place a graphic design and message that grab attention and provoke a response. Use the back of the business card to carry your mantra or company catchphrase. (Consider using your signature color as the background color and printing your slogan in white type.) Then use the brainstormer above to test your card's appeal.

THINK INTERNET

The minute you print a brochure, it is out of date. Production is expensive. Distribution is expensive.

A Website or a blog is a powerful way to create a dynamic brand identity and a community of loyal brand fans. You can express your interests or market your business with your own Website or blog. Or use the company Website or intranet to build visibility for your initiatives.

Websites are the ultimate branding. They can build a powerful visual and verbal identity quickly and affordably. They reach everyone you want to target and create a brand community. A Website allows you to display your brand personality and stay up-to-date and relevant. It allows you to be accessible to your customers or audience.

Look at Mark Cuban, the owner of the Dallas Mavericks, who made $1.9 billion selling his share of Broadcast.com. Cuban calls himself "the most accessible person in America" and always wants to hear from customers. He features his e-mail address on his Website, at his blog, and on the scoreboard at Mavericks' games.

It's important to approach Website design as powerful packaging and advertising for you, your business, or your ideas. Observe these 10 principles for developing a great Website or blog:

1. *Acquire a great domain name:* Reserve the most memorable URL you can get. It must be easy to remember and spell. Make it as short as possible. Think of domain availability when choosing your business name if you are a new entrepreneur. Even if you're part of a hosting Weblog, choose a URL that communicates your point of view or personality. You should always buy your own name.

2. *Have a clear focus:* View the top of the home page as the headline of an ad. Make sure you include an identifying phrase or tagline so that visitors will know immediately what the site is about. Obvious? Maybe, but maybe it's not, given the difficulties many visitors face with trying to figure out what Websites are selling or promoting. And choose all the possibly relevant metatags so that your site will turn up on Web searches.

3. *Have a distinct brand look:* You have just seconds to make a first impression, so be sure your site has a great look. *Don't use a template design.* You'll look like everybody else—like a generic, not a brand. Keep it simple and uncluttered. Find inspiration for your

> **A Website or blog is worth a thousand brochures.**

Web designer by cruising around the Web and looking for sites that appeal to you.

4. *Have a different message:* Use short, pithy copy, but *say something*. Too many Websites are full of jargon or don't say anything at all. Your Website is your chance to sell, so present your USP, your unique selling proposition, as something different from what everyone else is saying.

5. *Convey a brand personality:* Use color, design, imagery, graphics, and verbal messages to create a brand personality. Write in a personal style that engages visitors and builds a Web community.

6. *Use a dominant color:* Or use a distinctive palette so that you own a color or color scheme with which to build a distinct visual identity.

7. *Avoid clever navigation designs:* Sometimes navigation routes are hidden in the most unlikely places. It may be clever on the part of the Web designer, but if people can't navigate your site easily, they will move on.

8. *Use rich media sparingly:* People are busy, and rich media will slow down too many of them. Others don't have the tech savvy or computers to handle rich media. If you use it, have it as an option instead of opening your Website with it. It may be cute the first time people use your site but will probably be annoying after that.

9. *Link only to sites with compatible brand images:* Linking is a good idea, but link only to sites that complement what you do. Make sure you like the site and its brand image. If you align yourself with junk sites, you will pull down your brand.

10. *Solicit interaction:* Empower your visitors with the ability to get more information through links and subject areas throughout your site. Ask for visitor feedback. Have calls to action so that people may sign up for your e-zine or newsletter, make a sale, or solicit information.

CREATE EXPERIENCES

Don't stop with your person or your brand-marketing materials when you think of visual identity.

Think of *total brand experience*.

Today, marketers spend a lot of money creating a branded environment at the retail level. The point is to control the way customers experience the brand. Whether it's drinking a latte in a Starbucks or shopping at Victoria's Secret, the whole store environment is one big brand package. Retail employees are carefully selected and trained so that they are *brand ambassadors*. These branded environments are a very effective way of promoting the brand and building a loyal customer base.

> *The play's the thing.*
>
> **William Shakespeare**
> *Hamlet* (II, 2)

That's why you should think of brand experience too. Look at your clients and colleagues as customers. What is your brand experience like? How is your phone answered? Do you send your secretary out to meet a guest, or do you do it personally? Make sure that your brand experience is consistent and represents what you want to be known for.

THINK BRAND ENVIRONMENT

Your office is a part of your packaging and brand experience. Your office says a lot, so why not put your personal brand on it?

Even if you have standard corporate-issue furniture, consider accessorizing your office, as many people do. Bring in a handsome lamp, hang your Audubon prints, or even display your baseball memorabilia. The *Wall Street Journal* has a weekly column called "Workspaces" that features people and their offices. Read it over time, and you will see the range of inventiveness people use to create a branded work environment.

If you are an entrepreneur, you have more latitude in creating a branded experience. You want your office and business environment to convey the right brand experience, not a message that undercuts your brand.

Some CEOs and other senior executives nowadays take the opposite route and downscale. And that can be very powerful branding and good PR indeed.

Few executive moves can top joining the cube culture if they hope to communicate the feeling of a democratic work environment, where everyone is in it together. Wall Street has long had a bullpen, an open-plan workspace for the trading floor, where managers sit alongside their staffs. New York City mayor Michael Bloomberg, who came from that culture, has gotten a lot of ink by giving up the traditional, large mayor's office and moving into a bullpen-style space.

When technology companies such as Intel adopted the open-plan workspace with the CEO in the midst of the rank and file, they pioneered the trend on a broader scale. This arrangement has become the trademark of the just-folks, down-home style of eBay CEO Meg Whitman and is a big part of the company's empowerment culture.

THINK ADVERTISING

For your most important ideas and messages, you might want to take a big leap forward visually and study the advertising playbook. People aren't interested in messages and propaganda, but they are interested in being entertained or in learning something new that's important and relevant. That's why advertisers disguise their messages to make them entertaining or educational in TV commercials, print ads, advertorials, and Web games. Sometimes they even embed their products within the story line of a television show.

Rather than rely on a PowerPoint slide or press release, think about how you can use bold imagery or even film or video to tell a story. The film *Last Best Chance* isn't really a movie, but it's packaged as a thriller to get people to pay attention to its message about nuclear terrorism. It was produced not by a movie studio but by the Nuclear Initiative. It was distributed free of charge on DVD and also will be appearing on HBO. Presented as powerful "entertainment" with compelling visuals, the message got heard in a way that wouldn't have happened through conventional means such as press stories and talk shows.

STRIVE FOR A FOCUSED BRAND IDENTITY

Everything—business card, clothing, résumé, presentations, letterhead, holiday cards, office, Website, even your posture and gestures—conveys meaning, so use everything to your advantage.

What you want to do is burn in a single-minded identity at every touch point, producing a consistent brand experience. What you don't want to do is send confusing messages. That will undercut all your branding efforts.

But, remember, consistency doesn't mean cookie-cutter and identical. That's boring and rigid.

> **Branding always involves sacrifice.**

Marketers must always be prepared to give up a design or an attribute that could be confused with that of a competitor.

Eliminating such items enables you to distill the vital points that will give you a successful strategy with a focused message and presentation. You may have to leave out things that are off-strategy and would dilute or confuse your self-brand message.

What you want is a total brand experience that's consistent and powerful—that's you.

<< IN A NUTSHELL >>

The sixth secret of self-brands:

Create a total brand experience.

Make sure every touch point

has a consistent and special brand look.

HARNESS THE POWER OF NAMES, SIGNATURE WORDS, AND PHRASES TO LOCK IN YOUR MESSAGE

> *How long a time lies in one little word!*
>
> **William Shakespeare**
> *Richard II* **(I, 3)**

The words you use can be powerful and memorable or blow away like a feather in the wind.

Fresh or unusual words and expressions make you pause. You take notice of them. They create visual and verbal connections. They linger in your consciousness and may even work subliminally to create a brand image.

What if President Franklin Delano Roosevelt had not crossed out the phrase "world history" and replaced it with "infamy" in his famous lead sentence, which began "Yesterday, December 7, 1941, a date which will live in infamy"? One little word. But what a difference! The use of this unusual word made Roosevelt's phrase arguably the most famous ever uttered by a U.S. president.

Words can be so potent that what you create in the mind through words and messages often comes true. That's the power of advertising. Or the power of self-talk, whether it's positive or negative. Words can have a strong influence on your outcomes.

CREATE INTELLECTUAL CAPITAL

As a nation, we used to make things. Now we make ideas. We create intellectual capital. You need to make some, too, if you want to get ahead and build a strong self-brand.

When you look at public companies, it's clear that a large part of their value or market capitalization is due to brand. Today, soft things like brand names, slogans, trademarks, patents, and other forms of intellectual capital are often worth more than tangible assets like product inventories and bricks and mortar.

So, how do you create intellectual capital?

Branding shows you how.

Think *productize*. You start by packaging your ideas, projects, or services just as branders package names, messages, and catchphrases. Names and positioning slogans turn an intangible into a product or a brand.

A great name or slogan makes a good first impression, and it might be indelible if it is a particularly good one. Giving your projects or ideas a name and slogans draws attention to them and makes them seem more important.

Your ultimate goal as a self-brand is to achieve *memory lock*. You want your projects, capabilities, and persona to be noticed and get locked in the memory of your target audience.

BRAINSTORM IN CURSIVE

When you're trying to create names and coin expressions for your ideas, write down what comes to mind first.

Don't worry about whether an idea is good or whether it makes sense. Doodle with the words. Build one idea off another. Try not to filter your ideas. Your goal is to start creating intellectual capital and creative ideas for yourself.

Words without thoughts never to heaven go.

William Shakespeare
Hamlet (III, 3)

When you do this sort of brainstorming, try writing down your ideas in cursive. (You should already be doing this for the brainstormer exercises.)

Why?

Writing in cursive spurs the thought process. You actually come up with more ideas. You tend to probe things more deeply and be more creative since writing taps into your right brain, into your creativity and intuition. (If you type your ideas and responses on your laptop, print them out double-spaced so you can revise and add to them by hand.)

MAKE A NAME

A great name is a valuable asset. A name is a label that identifies and defines something.

> **From a branding perspective, the most crucial decision is the name of the product.**

A great name can practically make a brand. In fact, in some cases, there is not much difference between two products except for their names. The positive and negative feelings people have about a brand often reside in its name.

A name is critical for a brand because of its influence on a brand's image.

Consider these two cars. The Toyota Corolla and the Geo Prizm were the *same product*, manufactured as a Toyota and General Motors joint venture. Both cars were built in the same factory.

The only thing different about the cars was their names. One was branded Toyota Corolla and the other Geo Prizm (later Chevrolet Prizm). One commanded a premium price and sold many more cars each year.

Because consumers feel the brand-name Toyota is superior to the brand-name Chevrolet, Toyota could charge more and sold more even though the only difference between the two cars was the name. The Toyota name alone was worth many hundreds of dollars more per car and drew more consumer interest.

Finally, General Motors had to throw in the towel. The Prizm isn't made anymore.

LOOK AT YOUR NAME

Do you have a good name?

It may be unfair—after all, we don't choose our names—but your name often creates the first impression people have of you. (This is absolutely true if you aren't meeting in person.) And that first impression has a powerful influence on the lasting impression people have of you.

Names are just as important for people as for products. In one study, a researcher showed pictures of two beautiful women to a group of men. The group voted and ranked both women as equally beautiful.

Then, the researcher told the group that the first woman's name was Elizabeth and the other woman's name was Gertrude. Again, a vote was taken. This time, one woman had a 30-point lead in the beauty contest. And it sure wasn't Gertrude.

Social scientists call this "expectancy theory" or the "Pygmalion effect." If you have a name that's considered unattractive, people don't expect you to be attractive, despite what they see.

To a large extent, you see the image that the words trigger in you. So a name is either an asset or a liability.

BE AWARE OF NAME EXPECTANCY

A name may say whether you are rich or poor, native or foreign, likeable or distasteful, attractive or unattractive.

Steven D. Levitt and Stephen J. Dubner did an interesting study of names in their book *Freakonomics*, using California data that include not only each baby's name and vital statistics but detailed information on the mother's income, level of education, and date of birth.

Levitt and Dubner were able to categorize the "whitest" girls' names (Molly, Amy, and Claire) and the "blackest" girls' names (Imani, Ebony, and Shanice), as well as the "whitest" boys' names (Jake, Connor, and Tanner) and the "blackest" boys' names (DeShawn, DeAndre, and Marquis).

One interesting finding was the relationship between a baby's name and the mother's economic status. Another was the tendency of people with clearly black names to have a less advantageous life outcome than people with clearly white names. For example, the authors relate audit studies in which identical résumés were mailed out, one with a name that sounds white and one with a name that sounds like a black or minority name, and the résumé from the supposedly white candidate generated more interviews.

CREATE A BRAND-WORTHY NAME

A great last name certainly is worth something in business, your career, or your life.

We've all seen how having a famous last name like Kennedy, Bush, Rockefeller, or Hilton gives a person a big head start.

Just look at the offspring of celebrities or well-known people from the world of politics, business, or entertainment who are leveraging the family name to enter the family business or set up a different high-profile endeavor.

But if you're like me and most other people, you weren't born with a family brand name. You have to make a name for yourself. You must build your own brand, whether the realm is your community, your industry, your company, or the whole planet.

You will find it easier to build a self-brand if you have a good name. It's the same for products and for people: a good name is distinct—not too common or owned by someone else—and is easy to spell and remember. Of course, you also want a name with that something extra that will give you marquee name potential.

The image-making power of names is why a lot of people in entertainment, fashion, or other highly visible fields change their names. So Esther Lauder became Estée Lauder. Susan Weaver became Sigourney Weaver. And Paul Hewson became Bono.

Of course, you've reached the name zenith when your first name alone is sufficient to identify you, like Bono or Oprah, or when a single letter of the alphabet, like W, does the trick.

There has been a reemergence of the personal name as brand across all types of products and services. It allows for the development of a *brand character* based on what we think of as the individual's persona. You get two for one. You don't just have the brand; you have the person and the brand. Sometimes it's hard to figure where one stops and the other begins.

Different names create different assumptions.

Ralph Lauren is a familiar example. First, there's the name change. Would his success have been the same if his brand had been known as Polo by Ralph Lipschitz? I doubt it. Lauren needed a name with the right pedigree so that he and his designs could symbolize the Polo brand concept: hyper-WASP American aristocracy. And Lauren, the person, is the model for the look, lifestyle, and essence of the brand, symbolizing both the brand and its users.

Or look at Sean "Diddy" Combs, the former hip-hop performer turned business impresario. Combs is also a brilliant naming tycoon. There are the serial personal nicknames: Puff Daddy, Puffy, P. Diddy, and now simply the one word, Diddy. And there are the well-named product lines: Sean John for his clothing label and Bad Boy Records for his music label.

In another example, struggling author Joanne Rowling took her editor's advice and added a dollop of mystery to her persona by using the initials J. K. in place of her first name. (The "K" came from her grandmother, Kathleen.) And thus J. K. Rowling, the creator of *Harry Potter*, was born.

> *I would to God thou and I knew where a*
> *commodity of names were to be bought.*
>
> **William Shakespeare**
> *Henry IV* (I, 2)

The good news is that our ideas about what is considered a good name are evolving. It used to be a rite of passage for aspiring actors and actresses to change their names if they thought that doing so would be helpful for their careers.

Arnold Schwarzenegger wasn't held back by his name (although it breaks the rules of a good name by being too long, too ethnic, and difficult to spell). And "odd" first names are in vogue. No doubt Gwyneth Paltrow's daughter Apple and Julia Roberts's twins Hazel and Phinnaeus won't be hampered by their given names. Now it will be much easier for people to have unusual names and succeed. Brainstorm your name in the exercise on p. 104.

AVOID GENERIC NAME SYNDROME

Some people change their names to rid themselves of an overly ethnic, difficult, or ugly-sounding name. But many people have the opposite problem. If you have a name like Mary Jones or Bob Smith, you have generic name syndrome. You will likely find it more difficult to build a self-brand identity than you would if you had a more distinctive name.

Having a different name that is ownable in the category is critical. Brands trademark their names so that they own those names. That way, a competing brand can't use the same name or one that could be confused with it.

Here are some ways to make your name a better asset:

> *Use your middle name as your brand name:* Ray Charles Robinson became Ray Charles. Thomas Cruise Mapother IV became Tom Cruise. Angelina Jolie Voight became Angelina Jolie (Jolie means "pretty" in French, which gives the name a foreign flair as well.)

> *Use a quirky nickname:* An unusual or descriptive nickname is a great branding device. Think of Tiger Woods, Tipper Gore, and Topher Grace.

> *Use your full name:* A middle name often makes a generic last name stand out. Sarah Jessica Parker, James Earl Jones, and John Fitzgerald Kennedy are good examples.

> *Use a double-barreled last name:* This works best if the last names are short, for example, Catherine Zeta-Jones.

<< BRAINSTORMER >>

What Does Your Name Say?

Write your name on a piece of paper.

What adjectives or imagery comes to mind when you read or say your first name?

Which other people with this name come to mind?

If you could choose your name, would you choose this one?

If not, which name would you choose?

Is your name distinctive or similar to others? How could you make your name more distinctive?

How could you make your name suit you better?

> *Use initials:* Initials help you stand out: Jennifer Lopez is a fairly common name, but she also has the brand-name J-Lo to set herself apart. The poets T. S. Eliot and e. e. cummings successfully employed this device, as does J. K. Rowling today.

> *Spell a common name in an uncommon way:* Tune up a common name with a simple spelling change. Examples are Barbra Streisand and Suze Orman.

> *Hang your hat on one name:* This tactic is used mainly in entertainment, sports, or the arts but can be the ultimate in branding, such as Cher, Bono, Oprah, and Diddy.

> *Modify to add flair or a foreign accent:* Simply changing a few letters often makes an important difference. Gary Keillor changed his name to Garrison Keillor.

> *Simplify your name:* Many people chop off part of a name that is long or difficult to pronounce. James Baumgarner became James Garner, Antonio Benedetto became Tony Bennett, and Jennifer Anistonopolous became Jennifer Aniston.

> *Totally make it up:* This is the favored route of rappers and some entertainers. They give themselves names that are radically different from traditional standards, such as Ice Cube, 50 Cent, and the like.

> *Make a "bad" name work.* Today it's easier to break the rules and still succeed, especially if the name has a quirky quality, such as Renée Zellweger.

LOOK AT LABELS

Your name isn't the only word you need to think about. What "label" do you use when you describe who you are or what you do?

A label is an important naming word, too. Labels are names that define and position something in the minds of others. The way you label yourself can make or break you.

Different labels carry different perceptions.

A number of research studies bears this out. The Tufts University psychologist Nalini Ambady did a study showing students a two-second video of a professor. One group was given the label "statistics professor." The other was given the label "humanistic psychology professor."

Students described the statistics professor as "cold," "rigid," and "picky." They called the humanistic psychology professor "warm" and "concerned with students."

Both groups of students saw the same professor in the same video; only the job title was different.

So it's not surprising that more people have started looking at the labels they use for themselves. Hoping to expand the definition or escape the poor image contained in their label, stockbrokers became "financial consultants," used-car salesman began to call themselves "pre-owned vehicle consultants," and computer programmers became "e-business solutions experts" or "systems analysts." Countrywide Financial Services chief executive Angelo R. Mozila recounted in a *New York Times* interview that he no longer refers to himself as a mortgage guy when he meets someone new on the golf course. "Now I say I run a financial services business," he said. "I don't know why. It makes me feel better. I guess status."

TAKE TITLE

Whether or not you get the boss to change the job title on your business card, you should think about it.

Don't think a job title is cast in stone, either.

When I worked on Wall Street, my title initially was Senior Vice President, Director of Advertising. During a downturn in the market, which also affected the firm's ad budget, I created a community-based, cause-related marketing program. It had a lot of impact with a budget that was relatively small compared to the cost of TV ads. I approached my boss about changing my title to Director of Advertising and Community Affairs. This gave me a label that offered a bigger brand footprint and might open up more options in the future.

The following brainstormer will help you explore your own possibilities.

The corporate title is the other big label in business that ranks you as succinctly as the number of stars on an army general's shoulder. It matters whether you are branded a vice president, a senior vice president, or an executive vice president or have no corporate title whatsoever. Your

‹‹ BRAINSTORMER ››

What's Your Line?

What is your job title?

Is there a better way to label what you do or who you are?

title affects the perceptions people have about how you perform on the job and what you are worth.

So, as long as you are in a company or line of work that uses title branding of that sort, fight for the best brand label you can get. Or, move into an area where merit is measured in other ways.

OWN A KEYWORD

Brands try to own a word, or a short phrase, in the minds of consumers. If they succeed, people think of the brand when they hear the word. For example, "overnight," is identified with FedEx, "cola" with Coke, and "safety" with Volvo.

Owning a word is important because it means that your brand is positioned with an important attribute in the minds of prospects. Your brand has meaning in a world where there are so many brands and messages that most do not stand for anything. It's like being the dominant response that comes up when you enter a keyword in a search engine.

Owning a word helps self-brands too. Your word could be a positive attribute that defines you. It could be a niche in the market that you dominate, or it could even be an idea or point of view that people associate with you.

Many people end up owning a word by writing a book, as Tom Friedman did with "flat," Larry Bossidy did with "execution," Tom Peters did with "excellence," Al Ries and Jack Trout did with "positioning," and Jay Conrad Levinson did with "guerrilla."

As a celebrity CEO, Jack Welch didn't need to increase his renown by writing a book (though he may have wanted to do some brand polishing after a messy divorce). But with his publishing success, he laid claim to the word "winning."

SELF-BRAND KEYWORD: A signature word or keyword is a word that is closely identified with you and defines you in an important way. It helps catapult your self-brand.

You might choose to own a word that expresses an important attribute you believe in, as Benjamin did with "accountability." He used "accountability" in talking about his vision for the company in internal meetings, in memos, and on the company Website.

Benjamin also took action to embed "accountability" in the culture and associate the word with his leadership. He introduced new sales reporting metrics and performance reviews and instituted client feedback mechanisms and similar procedures that tangibly demonstrated accountability in action.

NAME YOUR IDEAS

Business doesn't have to be just about facts and statistics. And it's not smart branding if that is the way you approach it. You have to create interest in what you have to offer, not bore people. That's why smart businesspeople, like smart brand managers, brand their ideas by packaging them with a name.

> *The poet's pen . . . gives to airy nothingness*
> *a local habitation and a name.*
>
> **William Shakespeare**
> *A Midsummer Night's Dream*

Naming is a good way to create tangible assets for your self-brand. Naming an important idea or project has enormous advantages. When you give something a name, you make a tangible thing out of an intangible. A name will help people visualize and understand your idea or the point you are making.

Names make your ideas and points more memorable. When you name something, you are branding it and giving it the potential to be a "big idea." Names will help you sell your project to your clients, whether external or within your organization.

Coining your own word or expression gives you a marvelous branding device for both your idea and yourself. If you express your key message in an interesting way, it helps people see your point of view and makes you more memorable.

MAKE IT STICKY

Give your idea or point an unusual or quirky name. Quirky words are sticky—they stay in the mind, and people remember them.

In the 2004 presidential campaign, President George W. Bush used the sticky expression "flip-flopper" to brand John Kerry. If Bush had simply said that Kerry changes his position a lot, it wouldn't have had the same impact with the media or with voters.

Look at the names of two current business best-sellers. Many of us probably thought of economics as "the dull science" until the name *Freakonomics* defied that label and grabbed our attention. Then there is Tom Friedman's book *The World Is Flat*. Friedman got the idea for the book after an Indian businessman pointed out how technology was leveling the playing field between East and West. Friedman could have stopped there and titled his book *The Level Playing Field*. While the arguments in the book would have been the same, the book wouldn't have had all the sizzle or the scariness that the name *The World Is Flat,* brought. Also, "flat" was a fresh word that Friedman could "own." ("Level playing field" had already been used too much from a branding perspective.) Friedman has shown a brander's sensitivity to naming ideas throughout his writings, coining names like "Globalization 3.0."

Give your idea a particularly memorable name or a name with emotional content, and you can create a company rallying cry. At GE, Jack Welch used the word "boundarylessness" for the idea of employees finding good ideas everywhere and sharing them throughout the company. Welch could have simply said "idea sharing," but it wouldn't have had the same impact. Though awkward and a bit of a tongue twister, "boundarylessness" was unusual and unexpected. It was sticky.

You can persuade people to your point of view with the names you give things, particularly options in a series that are under consideration. Henry Kissinger talked about "coloring the options" when he presented various alternatives for then president Richard M. Nixon to consider.

PLANT A BETTER NAME

You don't have to invent the big idea either when you're creating intellectual capital, although you should put your own spin on all ideas. If you give an existing idea a great name and spread the word, you'll end up owning it in the minds of others.

For example, the concept of ideas and trends spreading like an epidemic originally came out of the worlds of science and social science. One scientist, Richard Dawkins, called such ideas and trends "memes," probably not the best name if you want your term to spread.

Malcolm Gladwell wrote elegantly about the concept, coining the phrase the "tipping point" to describe ideas and trends building slowly at first and then dramatically tipping and becoming a mass phenomenon. When his book *The Tipping Point* made the best-seller list, the concept entered the national consciousness. And Gladwell gave good names to the people who tip things: connectors, mavens, and salesmen.

Seth Godin put his own spin on the concept. He came up with the term "ideavirus" and wrote a book called *Unleashing the Ideavirus.* (You are trying to create an ideavirus with the names you give your ideas.)

Godin took it one step further and came up with the concept of packaging your ideas to make them spread faster.

USE YOUR OWN NAME

The best place to start is often your own name. You make the history books if you get your name to stick to your idea, as with "Moore's Law" and the "Peter Principle." Or your name could become an adjective that describes your intellectual contributions, like "Darwinism," "Pavlovian," and "Freudian."

Look at the diet book category: Dr. Robert Atkins didn't invent the no-carb or low-carb diet. Others came before him; but he used his name for the diet and in 1972 came out with a book, *Dr. Atkins' Diet Revolution*.

Atkins had a fresh USP: if you cut out carbohydrates, the body will react by eating body fat. The USP and branding resonated with the public. Soon the name Atkins became synonymous with "no carbs" and "skinny." In the 33 years since it first came out, Atkins's book has sold a whopping 21 million copies.

TIP AN IDEA

Atkins ruled the low-carb diet world until Dr. Arthur Agatson came along. (His name may not be as familiar as Atkins, but his diet sure is.)

At first, Agatson named his diet "The Modified Carbohydrate Diet." He promoted it with a booklet in 1996 among a relatively small group of overweight clients in Miami, who started losing weight.

What propelled the Miami diet doctor to great success was a sexy name and packaging. Of course, he had a good product—a good diet—but there are a lot of good diets out there.

The doctor didn't use his own name, Agatson, which is a bit hard to remember and spell. He piggybacked his diet on the name and imagery of a chic part of Miami Beach when he launched his book, *The South Beach Diet*, in 2003. The book went on to top the best-seller list, spawned two spin-off books, and sold 14.5 million copies in two years. It was a phenomenal success.

Would the diet have done as well if he had continued to call it "The Modified Carbohydrate Diet"? Unlikely. Or if he had used his own name and called it "The Agatson Diet"? Again, unlikely.

A good name can make your idea.

A fabulous name can really make the idea break out.

The words "South Beach" gave the diet a memorable handle, like the Scarsdale Diet developed by Dr. Herman Tarnower. Only South Beach has more cachet and sexier imagery than Scarsdale.

An interesting by-product of the South Beach phenomenon was that the label "low-carb" also took off. Soon food companies started putting the words "low-carb" on thousands of products, both foods naturally low in carbohydrates and new low-carb versions of high-carb foods. And their sales also took off.

FIND ENTICING NAMES

Smart self-branders name their ideas all the time. The trend guru Faith Popcorn comes up with fanciful names for her trends, such as "cocooning," that put them (and her business) on the map. Ditching her ethnic last name and adopting "Popcorn" was her first naming feat.

If you are in a service business, avoid generic marketing of your services. Don't list capabilities and features. Package your services and name them so that you create excitement and can sell the benefits of what you are offering.

Look at hotels. Most used to market themselves on price per night. Now, smart hoteliers also use names and packaging to create demand. They offer "Romantic Couples Weekends" or "Mother/Daughter Spa Weekends" or "Fitness and Beauty Weekends." Small bed-and-breakfasts offer "Mystery Weekends" or "Civil War Battle Reenactment Days."

One of my clients, Lynn, first began coining words as a sales representative for a large pharmaceutical company. New government rules and guidelines dramatically changed the traditional way of selling to doctors. Pharmaceutical sales reps were no longer allowed to offer gifts, freebies, trips, or other perks to doctors.

Of course, reps like Lynn still had to get in the door and make sales if they wanted to stay employed. On top of that, there were more sales reps than ever. Lynn was just one of more than 100,000 sales reps tripping over one another trying to gain physician access.

She began focusing her sales efforts on the science behind the drug and created a sound bite, "Schmooze is out, science is in." Lynn started using her tagline at her company and with clients. Then, she began talking at industry conferences about the need for sales reps to *sell science, bring intellectual value,* and *build mindshare* with busy doctors in a highly competitive marketplace.

ENCAPSULATE THE NAME

When Lynn left the corporate world to start her own sales-training business, she wanted a way to market her workshops that expressed her innovative ideas on how salespeople need to sell today.

We came up with "Sell SMART." It is not a selling system. (Most selling systems are too complicated for salespeople to implement.) Sell SMART is a positioning line and uses an acronym that spells out the key ideas behind its selling philosophy. We completed the transformation by encapsulating the idea in a logo.

(**S**) . . . . . Find the **Sweet Spot**

(**M**) . . . . . Capture **Mindshare**

(**A**) . . . . . Have **Answers** and **Advice**

(**R**) . . . . . Get the Right **Reaction**

(**T**) . . . . . Think **Tactics**

With the new name and positioning, Sell SMART is now a brand in a sea of generic sales-training programs.

CREATE SELF-BRAND BITES

Mark Twain wrote literary masterpieces, but he was also a master of the sound bite. His ability to toss off an interesting phrase on important issues and life experiences brought Twain to the attention of people around the world.

Today, if you have a television show, you need a signature line, like Trump's "You're fired." And many hot shows spawn sound bites that take on a life of their own outside the show, such as *Sex and the City*'s "He's just not that into you."

SELF-BRAND BITE: Punchy expression of your idea or point of view. It should be short and memorable and have an element of the unexpected.

One of the jobs of a politician or pundit is to create catchphrases and labels that frame the debate or debunk naysayers. California governor Arnold Schwarzenegger did this with "girlie-men."

You should harness the power of defining phrases or catchy slogans for your ideas and your department or company mission. Don't give a presentation, make a new business pitch, or present a recommendation to your boss without three or four sound bites on your key points.

Sound bites are memory magnets. They could be surprising, shocking, or funny. They may use word play or other literary devices such as rhyme and repetition. A sound bite creates a strong visual image that brings the idea to life in a novel way. At the very least, a sound bite should be a pithy saying that communicates your essential message.

Often, the devices that make for a great sound bite are the same as those used by marketers in developing great taglines or slogans for brands. In the past, advertisers often put the brand slogan to music and created an ad jingle. Once heard, it was surprisingly difficult to get it to stop replaying in your head. Now, ad jingles are passé, although music or sound may still play a role. McDonald's uses the slogan "I'm loving it" and a five-note melody. The company even created a hit song for Justin Timberlake.

TELL STORIES

Beyond a name and sound bite, you must think of how best to talk about and sell your idea. Most people speak in generic or factual terms about their ideas and projects.

It's a lost opportunity!

Use stories and anecdotes. Stories have universal appeal. Successful brands use the power of stories and an evolving story line to keep people interested in the brand and its message. You should, too.

Stories bring your accomplishments and personality to life for people in a way that gets them involved in the narrative of what happened.

Stories bring characters to life through description and dialogue. They make the challenge and struggle seem vivid and real. Bring in good dialogue (quotes and sound bites). Build suspense in the way you tell what happened.

> *An honest tale speeds best, being plainly told.*
>
> **William Shakespeare**
> *Richard III* **(IV, 4)**

Look at the following themes from literature and movies and see if there is a way you can talk about your ideas in a more dramatic way:

> Against all odds
> The comeback
> The turning point
> Talent wins out

Stories are often built on a narrative construction of conflict, struggle, and final victory. For example, the personal-finance author Robert Kiyosaki could simply have told his philosophy of successful money and life management in his book *Rich Dad, Poor Dad*. Instead, he used a story about the conflict between the teachings of his father (the poor dad) and his friend's father (the rich dad), who gave him the low-down on how money really works in the world.

It turns out there may not have been an actual rich dad, as a reporter later found out. But the story of the conflict made Kiyosaki's book captivating. No doubt, many people could relate to having a poor dad, a loving parent who worked hard and saved but didn't know how to work smart and invest for himself, much less pass these valuable lessons on to his children.

Using stories in a presentation to sell yourself, your ideas, or your company is a type of *emotional marketing*: getting people interested in your ideas not just because of the facts but because they *feel* something about who you are and what you're talking to them about.

NAME YOUR IDEAS

If you want to become a successful self-brander, you have to get into the naming game for your ideas, initiatives, and business concepts. Keep these 10 naming principles in mind:

1. *Keep it short:* Small names act big when you promote the brand. They are easy to grasp, spell, pronounce, and remember, and being remembered is half the battle in branding. Many brand names have gone on a diet (Citibank became Citi, and Federal Express is FedEx). Some top global brands are as short as three or four letters (AAA, Nike, Ford). Some brands even have one-word taglines ("Always," "Enjoy," and "Real" for Coca-Cola), and many top-selling book titles are made up of a single word (*Winning, Freakonomics, Blink*).

2. *Look for verb, generic, or sound-bite potential:* You hit the jackpot when your name becomes the generic term for the category (Scotch tape, Band-Aid) or a verb (Xerox, Google). You could even aim for an expression that enters the vernacular ("Where's the beef?" "He's just not that into you").

3. *Use unexpected or quirky words or expressions:* sresh words and expressions are sticky—they are memorable and grab people's attention (axis of evil). Just one unexpected word can make an expression sticky ("It's the economy, *stupid.*").

4. *Tell a story or paint a picture:* Words and expressions that suggest or describe are very effective. Research shows that people remember suggestive or descriptive names because the meaning

is embedded in the name (cocooning, the tipping point, the world is flat). Baby Einstein, the video and book publisher, has a name that conjures up every parent's dream for a newborn. Likewise, don't use names that have poor visual imagery. Beaver College in Philadelphia changed its name to Arcadia University and doubled applicants.

5. *Position the brand or idea:* Position your brand or idea favorably against competitors. Look at how the U.S. military chooses names for wars and military operations that appeal to people and position the campaigns favorably (Operation Iraqi Freedom).

6. *Employ literary devices:* Look at what has worked in great literature throughout history. Alliteration is used frequently to burn in a name or idea (Six Sigma, Spin Selling). Other literary devices such as rhyme, repetition, assonance, and parallel construction are also very effective ("Ask not what your country can do for you, ask what you can do for your country").

7. *Connect emotionally:* Try to create a name or expression for your idea or product that resonates and connects emotionally with the people you are targeting ("Just do it" for Nike, and "Whassup?!" for Budweiser).

8. *Consider tying in your own name:* The ultimate in self-branding is to embed your name in the idea or cause you're promoting. It can work if you have a name that's easy to say and remember (Moore's Law, Peter Principle).

9. *Make sure it sounds good:* Think of how the name, title, or expression sounds when you say it. Is it melodic? Does it sound right for the brand personality or the idea? Is the word memorable? Does the sound of the word suggest the idea? The original name for the zipper was "separable fastener" before B. F. Goodrich renamed it.

10. *Make it stretchable.* The best names and sound bites are elastic enough to grow. Apple uses the prefix "i" for its products as a memorable naming device: iBook, iPod, and so on. Bill Maher's "New Rules" and David Letterman's "Top 10 Lists" are stretchable enough to be used again and again with different examples, even spawning books and imitation.

STUDY THE MASTERS

People often ask me, "How can I learn to use the power of words to build my brand?"

Study the new brand names, ad taglines, and expressions that enter the public consciousness. But, if you're looking for real inspiration, read great literature.

For me as for many others, Shakespeare is the writer who continues to offer inspiration. He never ceases to astonish me with the branding power of words. Shakespeare is so rich that I've relied on his words alone in the quotes throughout this book.

It used to be said that Shakespeare is quoted more than any source except for the Bible. Now that statistic is out of date. The Bible is number two.

Certainly, Shakespeare has risen to the pinnacle because his expressions and use of words are timeless. English would have been a different language without him.

Shakespeare achieved the ultimate in word branding power. His words speak to all people regardless of their status in life, just as when he wrote them some 400 years ago.

‹‹ IN A NUTSHELL ››

The seventh secret of self-brands:

Burn in your messages

and your brand power

with memorable names, words, and expressions.

LEARN TO SPEAK FOR EFFECT, NOT JUST FACTS

> *All the world's a stage.*
>
> **William Shakespeare**
> *As You Like It* (II, 7)

We're always onstage.

In business, meetings are the primary stage on which you perform. You're aware, of course, that your performance on that stage, your presentations and your appearance, will shape your business image as either a star or an understudy. Phone calls, voice mail, letters, and memos are also part of the business stage and convey meaning.

What is the point of communicating if you don't have an impact? The ability to sell yourself and your ideas—to communicate to another person, whether it is your boss, employee, or mate—is a critical skill for personal success.

And *how* you say something is just as critical as *what* you say.

How often do you go into important meetings or make important calls or give presentations without a persuasive message? Communication means persuading people to choose you for the job, buy your product or service, or promote you to lead the department.

Great communication equals great self-branding. On a basic level, your success in life and in business depends on the art of talking and communicating well. And the higher you go in business, the more public speaking will be part of your job description. A 2005 survey of 100 Fortune 1000 companies by Burson-Marsteller revealed that CEOs receive an average of 175 requests a year to speak at conferences.

HAVE SOMETHING INTERESTING TO SAY

Lack of communication skills holds you back from promotions and relegates you to the B list at your company. As you move up in a company, the ability to build confidence in your leadership is a crucial part of the job. And being able to articulate and sell your ideas in meetings is your primary method of doing that.

> *It is better to be brief than tedious.*
>
> **William Shakespeare**
> *Richard III* **(I, 4)**

Never go to a meeting without having something to say and knowing how you are going to say it. Remember, there is not a lot of demand for messages per se, but there is a demand for interesting messages.

> **Advertisers dress up their messages by making them entertaining, relevant, or emotional.**

Prepare *three points* in advance of every meeting. These points should offer new information that will appeal to the people in attendance. Whether we're now entering the "Knowledge Age," the "Creative Age," or the "Conceptual Age" (all have been predicted), it's important to empower yourself and add intellectual value in your job, no matter what it is. If you're a salesperson, it's more important than ever to understand your clients' business and bring new solutions. As an executive or professional, you need to help invent the new ideas that will carry the company forward. If you are the president or chief executive, you need to have a vision for where the company is going and why that is important. And everyone at every level needs to be able to communicate these messages and ideas.

GIVE GOOD MEETINGS

If you're like me and many others, you've often thought, "I could really enjoy this job if it weren't for the meetings."

As a person building your self-brand, you want to be known for great meetings. This is particularly true when you are leading the meeting and have more control. But even when you are not in charge, you'll want to navigate your way through them successfully. To do that, you must understand the hidden rules.

These are the four basic types of meetings that you will encounter again and again in business:

> The staff meeting

> The "I want something" meeting

> The "move the project forward" meeting

> The presentation meeting

Let's look at what characterizes each one.

Staff Meeting

We are all familiar with the staff meeting, the team update with your boss and all your colleagues. Prepare beforehand a short synopsis of your three major points on key projects or issues and why they are important. This is not the meeting for droning on about the nine projects in your group or the detail of your call to Harry in legal.

Never introduce an initiative that your boss has not already approved or argue for a project at the staff meeting. The keywords for staff meetings are "brief," "informative," "informal," and "collegial."

"I Want Something" Meeting

This meeting generally takes place with your boss or a small group of executives when you are seeking approval for something: a new project or initiative, a budget increase, or a promotion.

> **TALKING POINTS MEMO:** A bulleted one-pager for your eyes only that prepares you for important meetings and interviews. All the key points should be linked to make a compelling argument for your recommendation.

This is your time to showcase your persuasive skills and a well-thought-out rationale or plan of action. It helps to prepare a talking points memo beforehand. This memo is your practice sheet with bulleted points. That way you can build a logical rationale and have all the facts at your fingertips.

Don't forget to weave in stories or anecdotes that will help defend and sell your request with passion and supporting facts.

"Move the Project Forward" Meeting

This is a team meeting pulled together to launch a major initiative and follow it though until completion. Because this type of meeting is cross-functional, one person usually is selected to be the team leader.

If you are the team leader, make your command of this type of meeting a notable characteristic of your brand. Take charge of the agenda by keeping the discussion lively but moving forward without acting like a drill sergeant. (If you do, you'll get the job done, but you won't have any friends.) If you are a team member, be prepared to discuss your progress and provide a handout for the group if there are a lot of moving parts.

Presentation Meeting

This is the most important type of meeting if you have self-branding aspirations.

At this type of meeting, you will be presenting a proposal, pitching a new prospect, updating senior management on an initiative, or speaking to a large group on an industry topic or broader issue.

TAKE A CUE FROM PERFORMERS

A presentation is a performance.

Great presentations (like great performances and branding messages) come about by focusing on your audience.

Actors and performers often do a mental rehearsal along with other preparatory exercises before they go onstage. The goal is to get in the right frame of mind to give a peak performance. Take a few minutes of mental quiet. Visualize success before you go onstage to speak. Imagine walking confidently onto the stage. Imagine hearing your voice speaking. Imagine being witty and engaging. Imagine the audience's applause. You might even want to have a personal trigger word or mantra, a special word or phrase that speaks to you.

As you develop your presentation, think as actors do of *becoming the audience*. Rather than worry about yourself, think about the reaction you want to get from your audience. You could even visualize yourself as an audience member who has gotten involved in your ideas. Feel the warmth and energy of the audience. The technique of becoming the audience not only will relax you but will help you figure out what to say and how to say it.

Great presenters engage the hearts and minds of an audience. So speak colloquial English. Don't read your talk. Internalize it. You want to be confident that you know the message so that you can speak from the heart.

If you are to give a great talk, you must say something interesting. Think about hot buttons that will move people emotionally and hot buttons that will move people rationally.

> **A talk is successful not when everyone nods in agreement but when some agree, some don't, and some are transformed by what you say.**

No audience wants to be bored, so don't give your listeners just the facts, with no unexpected or emotional connection. Pull the facts together in a way people haven't heard before. Tell a story that gets people emotionally involved in what you have to say. Bring a prop. Above all, aim for a magic moment that will make your talk memorable.

TALK PERSONALLY, NOT FORMALLY

The trick to formal business communication, whether it's oral or written, is to make it sound informal. You need to build a relationship between a brand and a target audience. And you do that by being natural and engaging, rather than formal and business-like.

It helps if you think of your business communication as a conversation with a colleague. Carry on a conversation in your head as you compose your thoughts. Think in terms of friendly engagement. Break the habit of relying on business jargon and technical terms.

You could tap into various influences in developing your speaking style. Listen to people around you who speak well and might help inspire your style: your minister or rabbi, executives in your company, speakers at networking or industry meetings.

Watch media personalities on television. Pay attention to their techniques and see if you could adapt one or more for yourself. Listen to the rhythm and cadence of their words.

BOOKEND YOUR BEST STUFF

The most important part of a presentation is the beginning. You win or lose your listeners in the first 20 seconds.

Display stage presence when you enter. Stand tall with your weight evenly distributed. If you are nervous, a good entrance will disguise it.

Plan your opening gambit. Open a talk with something unpredictable, something that will immediately grab the attention of the other people in the room.

Use contemporary news, stories, anecdotes, or examples to make your points. Pick words that paint a picture. Unusual words will impress your ideas in the minds of your listeners. Great speakers use language artfully to brand their ideas with an audience.

You need to hook your audience with a surprising statistic, news, or anecdote. Whatever it is, it should evoke an "aha!" from the audience. Say something that is different from the usual view (or why bother?). Too many talks are rehashes of what's been said before.

You also want to end on a high note. Keep a surprise or special story for the end, so that you leave your audience wanting more. The end of your talk is as important as the beginning. It's the same in brand advertising. The beginning and end of a television commercial are carefully planned to capture attention and impart the brand message.

SLOW DOWN AND PAUSE

Leave space around your words by talking more slowly and pausing. Just these two things will make a dramatic difference in your presentations or any type of spoken communication.

> *I stand in pause where I shall first begin.*
>
> **William Shakespeare**
> *Hamlet* **(III, 3)**

Pause at important points, such as at the beginning, when presenting key ideas, or while telling a story. When you slow things down, you give your listeners the opportunity to hear your ideas and to comprehend them and become emotionally involved. It will also make you seem more confident if you don't appear to be rushing through your message.

Pausing gives you a chance to take deep, relaxing breaths.

Try to carry these speaking habits into all areas of verbal communication. Most people talk too fast at meetings, on the phone, or when leaving a voice-mail message. As a result, they undercut their effectiveness as communicators.

FIND YOUR VOICE

A voice is like DNA; it is unique and recognizable. If voice branding weren't powerful—if you didn't recognize and respond to the voices of Tom Hanks, Ellen DeGeneres, and Eddie Murphy—there would be no point in paying stars millions of dollars to do voice-overs in animated films.

Consider the way your voice sounds. Many people cultivate their wardrobes or their images, but they don't cultivate the voices they use every day.

<< BRAINSTORMER >>

Recording Your Voice

Record yourself talking and play it back. Listen to it.

What do you hear?

What does your voice say about you?

Record yourself again. This time, try to put more resonance in your voice by speaking from the diaphragm. Work on your inflection by practicing speaking at a lower pitch. Then think of ways that you could improve your voice and vocal delivery.

The voice is a potent branding device. You use it all the time in the cell-phone and voice-mail world of our business lives. What does the sound of your voice communicate about you? Is it consistent with your self-brand strategy? How can you make your voice a powerful branding tool?

People will brand you by the way you speak, sound, and present your ideas, and they will judge you and your ideas accordingly.

If you are not happy with the sound, pitch, or cadence of your voice, work with it. You'll find that people respond to a lower-pitch voice rather than a higher-pitch voice. Try to develop a rhythm that works best for you. The next brainstormer will get you started.

CUT BACK ON POWERPOINT

Too many presentations are like trial by PowerPoint: too many slides, too many words, too many points.

One of the problems with PowerPoint is that it homogenizes your message.

Everything looks the same, from headlines to bullet points. Even if you say something memorable, it will be hard for the audience to pick it out and remember it in a sea of similar-looking slides. Here are my pointers for an effective slide presentation:

> *Make you and your message the star, not the slides:* Fight the monotony by limiting your slides to those that dramatize your message.

> *Follow the 10/20/30 Rule:* In his book *The Art of the Start,* Guy Kawasaki advises people to limit themselves to 10 slides, 20 minutes, and 30-point fonts when making a pitch: "The fewer slides you need, the more compelling your idea."

> *Use pictures, diagrams, and illustrations:* Don't rely on just words to make your points.

> *Develop a brand look for your slides:* Put your logo on the master slide, add a signature background color, or have a graphic artist design a branded template that will set your presentation apart.

TAKE THE STAGE

One advantage of cutting back on the PowerPoint habit is that you'll no longer be hiding from your audience.

You'll be able to harness the visual cues of gesture, posture, and appearance that contribute as much as 75 percent to an audience's opinion of a speaker. After all, you must engage the audience if you want to build your self-brand. You can't do that if they don't experience you because they are busy trying to follow slide after slide.

> *Speak the speech.*
>
> **William Shakespeare**
> *Hamlet* (III, 2)

Take the stage and enter the room with energy and confidence. Make eye contact with your audience. If you aren't looking at the audience when you start to talk, you won't get your listeners' attention. The development of a relationship begins with eye contact and full frontal engagement.

John F. Kennedy was said to look at people first in one eye and then in the other, a technique called "planting." In a large group, you can isolate a few people to make eye contact with. You want each person to feel that you are talking directly to him or her.

Don't let paper come between you and the audience, either. Know the message well enough so that you don't need to read it. (You can always put notes on index cards and keep them in your pocket, or use your slides as triggers.)

Use gestures or any animating movement that's natural to you. You want to make the audience feel your passion.

It's very powerful to expand the space you take on the stage. Just walking around on the stage will captivate the audience, and the closer you get to the audience, the more impact you will have. John Chambers, the chief executive of Cisco Systems, likes to walk around on the stage and into the audience like a talk show host. People have labeled him one of the most dynamic corporate speakers in America.

Pay attention to the room size. Your aim is to build a relationship between you and the audience, no matter how big or how small. Always ask for a room that is just the right size for the group. You don't want a lot of empty seats, which will drain energy from the room.

DON'T NUMB THEM WITH NUMBERS

Too often, business presentations are a sea of statistics—bullet, bullet, bullet; number, number, number; pie chart, pie chart, pie chart. Unless you're speaking to numbers people, don't cite a lot of numbers. Focus on the important ones if you want them to be remembered. You can also bring numbers to life through several techniques:

> *Show and tell:* Read a customer letter or relate an anecdote that brings the statistic to life.

> *Use an analogy:* Compare the number to something tangible from everyday life that people can understand. For example, you could say that the cost of funding a project is less than the cost of supplying the coffee machine on the sixth floor for a year.

> *Put the number in a time context:* Use established data in your comparison. For example, explain that savings from technology has cut production cost to one-tenth of what it was just two years ago.

GIVE EXAMPLES

If you tell people something, they will tune out. But if you involve them in your idea by bringing it to life through examples, stories, and anecdotes, they will remember what you say. Simple stories and examples often make the difference between a memorable, attention-grabbing talk and one that is totally forgettable.

Remember, no one, not even businesspeople,

lives by numbers and charts alone.

When you are a presenter, make a major point and then tell a story or give an example so that people can see and feel what you mean. Talk about a specific project, the people involved, and how it worked out. Take your listeners through a case study so they can experience it secondhand.

STUDY THE ELOQUENT PRESIDENT

Need to improve your presentation skills?

Become a student of good speaking. Study good speakers at events or on television or even from history. Then develop and practice your presentation so that you have a powerful delivery. Pay special attention to how your talk will *sound* to the audience.

Abraham Lincoln is one of my favorite mentors in the art of speaking well. In *The Eloquent President*, Ronald C. White Jr. points out that Lincoln was "fascinated by the sound of words." Lincoln "wrote for the ear," while most politicians "write for the eye." Lincoln said the words and expressions out loud as he was composing a talk. And it made a dramatic difference.

> *Remembrance of things past.*
>
> **William Shakespeare**
> *Sonnet 30*

Lincoln wrote and spoke in plain talk. He used Saxon words and simple sentence constructions and avoided the Latinate words and flowery rhetoric that were popular at the time.

White points out that, while the average person speaks at 150 to 160 words per minute, Lincoln spoke at 105 to 110 words per minute. Once, when he was unable to get to Springfield, Illinois, to give a speech himself, he mailed the speech with the request "read it slowly."

Lincoln kept his talks and letters short. He was always editing to condense and shorten them. His second inaugural address still clocks in as the second shortest. There's a wonderful story about the photographer setting up to take a picture of Lincoln speaking at Gettysburg. Lincoln got up, spoke, and sat back down, and the photographer was still setting up his equipment. (The Gettysburg Address was about two minutes long.)

Lincoln incorporated many literary devices in his talks, such as parallel construction, alliteration, and assonance. He used the device of organizing in threes, or triplets ("of the people, for the people, by the people," and "We cannot dedicate, we cannot consecrate, we cannot hallow this ground"). He used words to create vivid visual images ("bind the nation's wounds").

PRACTICE, PRACTICE, PRACTICE

Another story about the Gettysburg Address offers a valuable lesson. We have all heard that Lincoln wrote the Gettysburg Address on the back on an envelope while he was riding the train to the battle site.

It is true that Lincoln was the last person to be invited to speak. He received the formal invitation just three weeks before the Gettysburg dedication. But, according to White, Lincoln may have been asked orally before that.

Nonetheless, Lincoln worked on his remarks for at least three weeks. And he kept working on his Gettysburg remarks until the final minutes before he spoke. Some of the most memorable parts of the address, such as "of the people, by the people, for the people," were phrases Lincoln had been exploring earlier in his writings and talks.

The Gettysburg Address was not written spontaneously on the back of an envelope in a flash of brilliance.

No one, not even a person known for eloquence, like Lincoln, writes and delivers memorable talks without lots of preparation and practice. It's the case with all great speakers and presenters. Winston Churchill's secretary said that he spent 1 hour in preparation for every 1 minute of a speech. That means he would spend 30 hours preparing for a 30-minute talk!

GIVE RIVETING BACKSTORY

Perhaps the most riveting thing you can do with an audience is share personal stories and anecdotes about your struggles and triumphs. Steve Jobs told three stories at the commencement address he gave to the 2005 Stanford University graduating class.

The first story was about "connecting the dots." Jobs talked about being adopted and dropping out of Reed College after six months, and auditing courses that gave him inspiration later when he founded Apple.

The second story was about "love and loss." Jobs talked about losing his job at Apple, the company he had founded and loved. His initial anger gave way to a new period of creativity as he founded NeXT and Pixar, and met his wife.

The third story was about "death." Jobs told how he had been diagnosed with pancreatic cancer earlier that year. He thought he would have just months to live, but the cancer turned out to be a rare form that could be treated surgically.

Jobs talked about how each of these experiences turned out to be the best thing that could have happened to him at the time. He learned that "your time is so limited, so don't waste it living someone else's life."

At the end of his talk, Jobs left his audience with an image and a wish. He talked about the *Whole Earth Catalog*, "one of the bibles of my generation." He described the cover of the final issue, a picture of a country road, "the kind you might find yourself hitchhiking on if you were so adventurous," with the words "Stay Hungry. Stay Foolish." "And I have always wished that for myself," he said. "And now, as you graduate to begin anew, I wish that for you. Stay Hungry. Stay Foolish."

In his address, Jobs tapped into the power of telling authentic stories, personal stories that were right for this audience since they were about identity and life choices, and success, failure, and renewal. Jobs framed the speech using the device of three—"just three stories." His words were so compelling that people started talking about the speech, so it spread by word of mouth. (I read it when it was reproduced in its entirety in *Fortune* magazine.)

FUSE A STYLE

The lesson of great speakers is to study great orators and presenters who "speak" to you and use the inspiration they give you to create something uniquely your own.

After his keynote address at the 2004 Democratic National Convention, Barack Obama explained the sources of his speaking style to Anna Deveare Smith: "I tap into the tradition that a lot of African Americans tap into and that's the church. It's the church blended with a smattering of Hawaii and Indonesia and maybe Kansas, and I've learned a lot of the most important things in life from literature. I've been a professor of law. I'm accustomed to making an argument. When I am effective, it's coming from my gut."

Humor is a great way to make your presentation indelibly your own— not using canned jokes, but telling about events in a humorous way.

If you can make them laugh, you can make them buy your ideas. Laughter builds rapport. Humor is a hard thing to do well, but like any presentation skill, the more you observe people who use humor in their speaking and the more you do it, the better you will be.

Fuse your own speaking presence out of your strengths and the stylistic devices and speaking styles that work for you.

SHARPEN YOUR POINT OF VIEW

In professional communications, it's important to bring more of yourself into the equation. People will be excited by your take on the facts and how you present your ideas. By bringing more of yourself and your ideas into the equation, chances are that your audience will not only understand what you are talking about but will listen and respond to what you are saying.

An effective way of standing out is to have a defining point of view (POV)—your own "voice," a self-brand POV. Great self-brands create a philosophy. And the bolder and less conventional your point of view is, the more riveting it will be.

SELF-BRAND POV: Your own mental angle on the world, with a set of values and a narrative that ties it all together.

It could be a point of view on your industry, where it's heading, and what needs to be done to attain future success. It could be about your customers and what you or your department could offer them that they are not currently getting. It could be about anything.

We all need to hear viewpoints that help us frame the debate on topics of interest. That's why many of us turn to certain commentators, columnists, or news outlets. In a way, a news bias is like a point of view, and we tend to gravitate to news sources with a point of view that supports our own.

In a 2005 paper, "The Market for News," two Harvard economists, Sendhil Mullainathan and Andrei Shleifer, studied the issue of bias in news and argue that people want more than accuracy. "Readers prefer to hear or read news that are more consistent with their beliefs," they point out. And they contend that news producers can use bias or a defining point of view as a marketing tool with which to differentiate and fight the competiton. In short, having a point of view increases consumer loyalty.

It will help you in your career, too; you will be viewed as a person with a point of view—a brand—someone who is different from the norm.

BRAND IT

You could use a provocative stance and personality as a defining stamp. Or introduce a signature element that becomes a trademark of your presentations. At the State of the Union address, the president acknowledges everyday American heroes who are present in the audience. It's become a branded element of the address.

Whatever your personal style, here are 10 guidelines for moving your presentations from good to great:

1. *Start out strong:* Your opening lines will make or break your presentation. So begin with dramatic news, a tie-in with a current event, or an amusing story that will grab attention. (President Kennedy surprised his audience when he began his talk at the Berlin Wall in German: "Ich bin ein Berliner!") Don't forget to make a strong entrance and show some stage presence. (Standing straight and evenly on both feet will go a long way toward building presence.)

2. *Use stories and examples:* Bring each point to life through an anecdote, a story, or an example. People remember stories. That's why parables and stories have been used throughout time. Give your audience backstory that fills in behind-the-scenes details or your personal struggles.

3. *Control the message:* Think strategically about the substance of your message. Develop a few key themes around a central point of view. What is the best way to affect this audience emotionally with what you want to say? What is the best way to persuade them rationally? Weave in both as you develop your themes.

4. *Brand it with your brand:* Let your personality and point of view come through. Make your talk indelibly your own through your presence, style, and way of speaking. Develop a branded element, such as a show-and-tell prop, to strengthen your point.

5. *Finish strong:* The ending is as important as the beginning. Think of a memorable takeaway phrase for your idea and leave your audience with it. Always end on a high note, so that the audience will want more. Use the question-and-answer period to repeat your message in a new way, not to get into new themes. Even if you're hit with a trick question, stand firm and answer with one of your key messages.

6. *Coin words and sound bites:* Harness the power of names and sound bites for key ideas and concepts throughout, so that what you say is unforgettable.

7. *Use the branding power of your voice:* Your voice can have a dramatic impact or undercut your message. Put resonance in your

voice by speaking from the diaphragm. Speak in as low a tone as is natural. Practice your speech out loud, record it, and listen to your delivery. Use emotion in your voice to underscore a point.

8. *Talk (don't read) to one person:* Think in terms of talking to one specific person, and you will be less likely to pontificate or to be overly formal. Don't let a written speech or slides come between you and the audience. Likewise, use the simple words and colloquial expressions that you would use in conversation.

9. *Pause and slow down:* Don't rush through a talk. Leave air around your key ideas so that you don't reduce or eliminate the impact of your lines. You should always feel that you are speaking too slowly when you are giving a speech.

10. *Offer something new:* How often have you sat through a presentation and thought "I've heard all that before"? Always bring some fresh content to your talk. Having a surprise—something bold the audience didn't expect—is even better.

Personal communication is a crucial skill for anyone embarking on the journey toward becoming a self-brand. It's a skill that few of us are born with. But we can all develop a wonderful personal style through practice.

> *Mend your speech a bit*
> *lest it mar your fortunes.*
>
> **William Shakespeare**
> *King Lear* (I,1)

After all, if you're not selling your recommendation, yourself, or your product, you've got to learn how to do it, fast. Otherwise, you're wasting everybody's time. You'd be better off just cutting to the chase and mailing in what you were planning to say. And that will have very little self-branding power.

‹‹ IN A NUTSHELL ››

The eighth secret of self-brands:

Cultivate a powerful communication style,

a voice that is heard

because of what you say

and how you say it.

BUILD A WIDE NETWORK
OF CONTACTS AND ASSOCIATES

> *Be wealthy in your friends.*
>
> **William Shakespeare**
> *Timon of Athens* (II, 2)

Successful people nurture a network of contacts. Ouch! This sounds calculating and heartless. So let's go past the words and look at an example we all know.

Once upon a time, there was a dynamic businessperson who didn't know he had something wonderful. He was just a small-town banker although he could have been more.

Business can be ugly, and an unscrupulous rival took advantage of a simple mishap to ruin him. Not realizing that he had tremendous assets, the banker fell into despair and decided to end his life.

After a failed suicide attempt and a very strange night, he arrived back home to find that his assets were there: his family, his contacts, his friends. His network had rallied to solve the problem.

Everyone cheered when his brother lifted a glass and toasted him: "To my big brother, George. The richest man in town!"

NETWORK ANYTIME, ANYWHERE, WITH ANYONE

You'll find the more people you know, the more opportunities will come your way, and the more help will be there when you need it. And the bigger your network gets, the more it will multiply and the more valuable it will become.

Real networking is about building relationships, and relationships lead to accessibility. The best way to network is to adopt the George Bailey model: help others and be genuinely interested in what they do and care about. You'll find networking a lot easier if you take the work out of it. You turn networking into a chore when your primary goal is making contacts and you think you have to drag yourself to meet-and-greet events to do it.

Adopt the George Bailey model. Everyone is a potential contact and resource if you are open, receptive, and helpful, too. And networking could take place anywhere, from waiting in line at an ATM, to chatting at an industry trade show, to parents' night at your kid's school. (Children are great connecters, as any parent knows.)

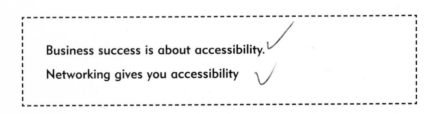

> Business success is about accessibility.
>
> Networking gives you accessibility

Robert is a busy executive in New York City, but he sets aside 10 minutes a day to call or e-mail business colleagues and acquaintances. Just 10 minutes first thing in the morning or between meetings. "My day is pretty much wall-to-wall meetings," he says. "Then there are the dozens of e-mails on my computer or BlackBerry. But I make the time because I can't afford not to. When I lost my job after 9/11, I found a new position though a networking contact. My network helped me rebound much quicker than other colleagues who were caught up in the financial services meltdown."

NETWORK FOR IDEAS

Move away from the idea that your goal in networking is to make useful contacts. Instead, decide that your goal is to expand your thinking, get new ideas for your work or life, and maybe make some lifelong friends in the process.

Just this shift in emphasis makes a big difference. You'll be much more successful at networking if your motive is to learn and get to know a wide variety of people, rather than to hustle contacts or business.

People can sense when you're genuinely interested in discussing ideas and experiences and when you're interested in knowing them just because they can help you.

That's why I say, *network to learn*. Don't network for contacts who will help you. You'll find it easier to build friendships and alliances that lead to more, whether it's an introduction to someone at a company you're targeting or a referral for a board seat.

When you take this approach, you'll also discover the value of knowing people with different backgrounds and from different areas of the world. You'll also become "information central" in areas of interest to you, an important role for any networker.

> If your motive is to learn and be involved, not to make contacts, you'll end up with more contacts.

INVEST IN YOUR NETWORK

When you take an interest in stretching your mind or getting to know people who share areas of interest, you'll have a network in place long before you need it. You may invest more than you get back in the early years, but over time the payback is enormous, emotionally and tangibly.

Knowing people is especially important today. Whether it's job security or job progress, you can't count on the company.

Recruiters can't open as many doors as a good network can, either. A recent Bureau of Labor Statistics study showed that more than 70 percent of executive jobs paying $100,000 or more were obtained through a friend, relative, or business acquaintance.

> *Society is no comfort to one not sociable.*
>
> **William Shakespeare**
> *Cymbeline* (**II, 2**)

You have to rely on the people you know and the people who know you. This is true no matter how talented, smart, and experienced you are.

FISH WHERE THE FISH ARE

Putting your network together will take some ingenuity at first, and then it will take some effort to keep it alive when you are busy. But first off, you'll need to put yourself in places where networking is good. These are the best networking places:

> - Industry conferences
> - University alumni groups
> - Networking groups
> - Gender- and ethnicity-based business groups
> - Nonprofit activities
> - Private clubs

BUILD A TWO-WAY STREET

A network is a relationship. It's a two-way street.

Some people view a network as a one-way proposition—something that you use when you need help. We've all had to deal with people who call only when they are looking for a new job or who give you a business pitch right after meeting you.

That is not networking. That is using people.

Here's how great networkers build a relationship and keep it alive:

> *Find common ground:* In order to take an introduction to the next level, you need to connect in more than a superficial way. Find linkages and areas of mutual interest with people of different backgrounds. This is what schmoozing is about. Always remember, you must connect to a human being so you have to take the conversation beyond small talk to something more personal and engaging.

> *Act like a host:* It can be daunting to go to a big event where it's hard to get an hors d'oeuvre, much less meet people you would like to meet. That's why a number of master networkers advise acting like a host yourself. Rather than waiting for someone to introduce you, go up to a group or an individual and introduce yourself. Most people will be wearing name tags, so it will be easy to break the ice by referring to their organizations or companies. And individuals who are standing alone will no doubt love you for it. Likewise, back home you can create events like a small dinner gathering at a local restaurant to bring together diverse people in your network.

> *Help someone first:* Make the first move to help the new people in your network, even if it's just forwarding an article via e-mail. Generosity pays. The benefit of giving first plays into what social scientists call the "reciprocity rule." People feel a need to do something for you when you do something for them first.

> *Take your business cards with you everywhere:* Most people make the mistake of not carrying business cards. Consequently, they don't have one to offer when they meet someone they want to get to know better. It's hard enough to remember a person's name and particulars—don't make it impossible by not having a card.

> *Keep the embers alive:* Send a short note or e-mail to a new contact right after you have met them. The embers will die if they aren't tended in the early stages of a relationship. Never let someone completely disappear from your network unless there is a good reason. Have touch points like periodic e-mail, holiday cards, and a surprise phone call.

> *They that thrive well take counsel of their friends.*
>
> **William Shakespeare**
> ***Venus and Adonis***

SEEK VARIETY

Great networkers don't just fish for the big fish, the senior executives and power brokers.

Networkers realize that you need a lot of different types of people on the road to success. Different folks bring different influences and abilities into play. Here are the special kinds of people who can play a powerful role in your professional network:

> ❯ *Grass roots:* This is your *core group*. Grassroots supporters are people—friends, family, business colleagues—who know you well and will do what they can to help further your success. What they lack in prestige, they make up for in the support they provide.

> ❯ *Rulers:* This is an important *power base* to nurture. Rulers are high-level executives at your company and elsewhere whom you know (although you may not know them well). Find graceful ways to stay in touch with these more experienced people through areas of mutual interest.

> ❯ *Connectors:* This group *leverages* your reach. Connectors are plugged-in people who know everyone. Connectors may or may not have powerful jobs. Doctors, financial advisers, and even hairstylists often are valuable connectors because they interface with so many different types of people. Bloggers are strong connectors, and the blogosphere is a great place to tap into a network of networks.

> ❯ *Promoters:* This group is your *PR machine*. Promoters amplify your self-brand message by word of mouth. They sing your praises and are invaluable in building your self-brand equity. One or two promoters in your network pack a lot of media power.

> ❯ *Gurus:* This is your *think tank*. Gurus are people such as mentors or professors whom you can call on for advice or strategy ses-

sions. They know a lot, are well read, and like nothing more than sharing what they know.

> *Weak links:* This is your *wild card.* These are people you don't know well but who could be consulted for advice or help. Don't ignore them. A weak link is often the source of a job lead that pans out. Most of my jobs were attained through a weak link, someone I didn't know very well or had just met though a friend. It's often a connection outside your usual networking circles that provides the entrée to the new arena you want to enter.

USE, DON'T ABUSE, YOUR NETWORK

Once you have your network, there are hidden rules to follow so you will not wear out your welcome. Many people ask for too much. Here are 10 top networking dos and don'ts to keep in mind:

1. *Ask for one contact:* Don't say, "I'm looking for a job in marketing. Do you know anyone?" The better way is to say, "I'm targeting the X industry or Y company. Can you suggest someone I could talk to?"

2. *Ask for something specific:* Don't be vague or too general. It's hard to respond to sweeping requests. Ask for help on one company, or ask the person in your network to do something specific (such as write a letter) and provide a time frame, if there is one.

3. *Ask for advice or a point of view:* Everyone loves to give advice, and this is always a great way to approach your network. It is a good way to lead in before asking for something more, such as an introduction.

4. *Tell the person you have everything lined up except for X:* Don't overwhelm your contact with too many requests. For example, tell a contact that you have written your project proposal and now just need to locate X or figure out Y.

5. *Keep the conversation upbeat:* Don't depress your network with your fears and problems. Don't share your anger about your company or boss, or your financial problems.

6. *Do your homework:* Find out the interests and backgrounds of the people in your network. Let them get to know who you are and

what you're like, but do your homework so that you get to know them as well.

7. *Thank people immediately:* Saying thanks at the end of the phone call isn't enough unless you have made a simple request. When people go out of their way to make an introduction, let them know how special they are for helping you by sending handwritten thank-you notes or letters.

8. *Keep people informed on the results:* Remember to tell the people who helped you that you got the meeting or the job you wanted. (Lack of follow-up is a complaint I hear frequently from people who went out of their way to help someone and never heard back about what happened.) Send periodic updates on your progress.

9. *Stay in touch:* A warm contact will grow cold if it is not nurtured. Keep in touch periodically through e-mail, phone calls, lunch, notes, or letters.

10. *Reciprocate:* Don't neglect to help people in your network. Stay tuned for things you can do to help your network. And, if someone asks you for help, follow through.

ENTER THE INNER SANCTUM

As we all know, there is a hierarchy of networking events and organizations. The by-invitation-only events and clubs are more powerful than organizations that are open to everyone.

At the pinnacle are private clubs or meetings like the World Economic Forum Annual Meeting at Davos, Switzerland, which attracts top CEOs and heads of state from around the world. Many elite organizations charge a hefty admission fee or require that new members be nominated by members. Even book clubs in some major cities are highly exclusive.

These are power networking events and organizations where the elite meet.

So how do you get in?

> **Strategic networking requires planning and homework.**

‹‹ BRAINSTORMER ››

Getting into the Sanctum Sanctorum

Think of an elite group or organization that you would like to join. Figure out which people in your network could be a link to the organization's gatekeepers, or determine how you can establish that crucial first link on the chain.

Through networking, of course. Strategic networking enables you to get to know people who know members of elite organizations. Then, you must network to build a relationship with the person who holds the key. Find common ground with the people you want to meet by researching their interests and backgrounds. You'll also need to research the organization and think about how you can bring value to it.

Even going to important gatherings and conferences entails strategic preplanning or you won't connect with the people you want to meet. If there's a project or area of mutual interest, e-mail or call the person to suggest setting up a one-on-one meeting beforehand. Most people will be flattered by your interest and respond favorably.

Make it a point to read the bios of the speakers and panelists provided at a conference or event. See if you have anything in common or have a mutual business interest that you could bring up during the cocktail hour. Or approach them and comment on their talks. You'll not only learn more, you might form a lasting friendship.

Networking is a skill that anyone can learn. Self-branders learn it because they know they can't succeed on their own. And having a wide group of friends, colleagues, and advisers around makes the journey a lot more fun.

<< IN A NUTSHELL >>

The ninth rule of self-brands:

Whatever you want to achieve,

whoever you want to know,

wherever you want to go on your journey,

use your network to get you there.

THINK IN TERMS OF EMOTIONAL ENGAGEMENT WITH YOUR KEY TARGET MARKETS

> *Look fresh and merrily.*
>
> **William Shakespeare**
> *Julius Caesar* **(II, 1)**

Powerful brands touch people. Brands today are not about the product but about the relationship between the brand and the target market. That's why today's brand managers put a lot of emphasis on *emotional branding, brand personality, market segments,* and *total brand experience.*

We form the strongest bonds with brands we like, identify with, and feel emotionally connected with in our lives. Powerful brands make us feel more in control, more self-assured.

Ad agencies even help their creative departments develop advertising by writing descriptive brand briefs that bring the brand virtually alive.

The brand brief also defines and describes the target market for the brand. The target market not only is described in demographic characteristics such as age, income, and geography but is brought to life through softer characteristics such as lifestyle, attitudes, and way of thinking. The creative people really need to get under the skin of the target market in order to develop effective advertising for the brand.

The goal is to build a strong emotional bond between the brand and the target market through all branding activities: packaging, design, advertising, and other marketing programs.

THINK IN TERMS OF MARKETS

Business success is built around relationships, too. Your success depends on what other people—your target markets—think of you. It doesn't matter who is "objectively" more qualified or talented. What matters is what the people making the decision feel about you and your abilities versus the other people you are competing with.

Think about all the people who are important to your brand—your boss, your clients, and your colleagues—in terms of target markets and follow these six rules of thumb.

Rule 1: Prioritize Your Target Markets

Most people make the mistake of defining the market too broadly. So they don't give the most important consumers of their self-brands any more attention and service than they give to their less important consumers.

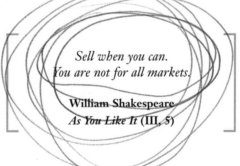

*Sell when you can.
You are not for all markets.*

William Shakespeare
As You Like It (III, 5)

In branding, markets are defined and prioritized. No one has the resources or time to go after everyone. No brand can appeal to everybody. Neither can you.

It's smart to pay more attention to the people who have the most impact on your brand's success. You want to create loyal customers by focusing on your most important customers.

Think in terms of primary and secondary markets:

> *Primary target market:* These are the key people who are the most important to your self-brand and who will deliver the best results for your brand. It could be your core group of clients and prospects. If you work in a corporation and don't have external clients, your boss and key senior executives may be your primary target market.

> *Secondary target market:* These people also have some impact on your brand and could become more important in the future.

Rule 2: Create Loyal Customers

As a self-brand, you want to do a terrific job with your target markets.

You want to turn them into loyal customers or even apostles for your brand.

There's a saying in branding that you know when a product becomes a brand when your customers are your salespeople. That's why branders put so much focus on building a community among their customers. And they strengthen community ties through loyalty marketing programs or friendship branding with special events and rewards programs for customers. Communities make brands thrive. And happy communities grow into bigger communities since the word of mouth is so positive.

To build a community of "loyal customers" for the brand You, you must understand what makes the people you are targeting tick. Marketers often do segmentation studies and give the segments names like "Actives," "Show-offs," "Family Values," "Worriers," and the like. These psychographic descriptors help marketers design sales and advertising messages. You might want to look at your target markets that way, too. What are they looking for? What values are important to them? Given this understanding, what is the best way to appeal to this group of clients or that senior manager?

If you were a competitor, how could you top your performance with your primary target market? What would your clients love you to do that you are not doing now? Start doing it.

What are the sore spots? What are you doing that they don't like? Stop doing it.

What changes can you make to increase your target market's level of satisfaction?

> *Love all, trust a few,*
> *Do wrong to none.*
>
> **William Shakespeare**
> *All's Well That Ends Well* (I, 7)

The more precisely you define the target market and its needs and desires, the easier it is to package yourself and develop the best solutions, messages, and approaches to satisfy those needs and desires.

Rule 3: Develop a Clear Value Proposition

In analyzing market segments, you're looking for an opportunity. With which group would you be most successful? What is the right self-brand strategy for this target market? What is your value proposition—what do you have to offer them that competitors don't?

If the target market is defined too broadly, your value proposition won't resonate with anyone because it will be too broad and vague. It will be impossible to build a strong brand identity, too. Your image will be too general to attract interest and loyalty.

In attacking a narrow target market, you need to make sure the segment has enough size and growth potential. You want to own a valuable target market niche.

Say you are a financial consultant targeting women. Which women are your best prospects? Women differ in age, income, education, lifestyle, marital status, geographic origin, and psychology.

Even women with high net worth may be too broad a target market. Maybe it's high-net-worth female executives and entrepreneurs. Or it could be women who are divorced or are planning to divorce. Or maybe it's widows. Or it could be women who have inherited money.

Each of these target markets has distinct needs and interests that would not be satisfied with an approach that targets the broader market of women in general.

Rule 4: Build an Emotional Bond

Today, brand managers put such a strong emphasis on emotional branding because people form the strongest relationships with brands they like and care about.

It's often the emotional ties that bind. Rationally, we often can make a case for why the capabilities of one company are better than another's or why one person's experience is superior to that of another. Yet our gut may tell us something different. We choose the one that makes us feel more comfortable emotionally.

Your goal as a self-brand is also to build satisfied and loyal customers, people who have good things to say about you because they have strong feelings about you, too.

One simple thing to keep in mind will go a long way toward building a strong bond with your target markets: Listen more and talk less.

Listening seems so simple, yet few have mastered the art. Listening helps in building strong relationships and engaging your target audience. When you listen rather than talk, you flatter your audience. You'll create a great impression (and learn a lot at the same time).

When you listen, you are telling people that you think they are smart and worth listening to. You are saying that you care about their concerns, that you feel something for them. Listening also says that you are the type of person who wants to learn and improve.

It's so simple and so powerful. By simply listening, you often engage your target markets more profoundly than by saying something profound.

Rule 5: Think Outside-in

A cardinal rule of branding is to think first of what reaction you want from your target audience (outside), then figure out what you have to do to get that reaction (inside).

So don't begin with what you want (inside-out). Begin with what you want your target audience to do, then plan your action. For example, if you are a salesperson, the reaction you want, of course, is a sale. But if you go right into a sales message with a new client, you probably won't get the reaction you want. Most people don't want to be sold, but they do want to buy. A better tactic is to get to know what the client's needs are and avoid "selling."

Think in terms of *framing* your message. People are different and what would work with one sales prospect (or any target group) might be completely wrong for another. Frame your message and how you act so that you connect with people's wants and desires. You want to connect with their "bias," what's important and relevant to them.

Rule No. 6: Attract Through "Soft Power"

The term "soft power" was coined by Joseph S. Nye in a book about how to attract people to your ideas in the arena of world politics. We're all familiar with exerting power through the carrot (paying someone) and the stick (threatening someone). Soft power is the third way. It is using things like your values, style, and point of view to attract others to you.

As I've said, branding shows you a lot about how to develop a style and point of view and other soft power ideas. One thing to think about that will increase your ability to attract others to you is executive presence. An important component of executive presence is bearing—the way you inhabit space. How do you enter a room? Do you stand tall and walk purposefully? Do you make an entrance? Or do you slouch and look distracted? Something as simple and controllable as bearing, your posture and stance and the way you move, is a powerful self-branding device that signals a lot to your target audience.

The other important component of executive presence is comportment—your way of conducting yourself when interacting with others. It's knowing how to greet and make conversation with new people at an industry event. It's knowing how to lead a meeting or handle an irate client. It's knowing how to behave in expected and unexpected situations, regardless of how many eyes are on you.

Now, let's look at the people in your target markets.

GUESS WHO'S NUMBER ONE?

If you work in a company, your boss is probably your number one target market.

Why?

Your boss has the most control over your self-brand (unless you have an internal network that's better than your boss, or very loyal external clients, or are related to someone important).

Look at Zoe's story. Warm and engaging, Zoe had an impressive background in brand management at well-known packaged goods companies. Unfortunately, she had spent her career building brands for others and had not done much to build her brand. Here she was, in her early 40s, unable to get to the next level although she had been with the same company for 8 years. She worked hard and had a loyal team, yet some colleagues with similar experience and levels of responsibility had been promoted to vice president, two levels above her.

What was she doing wrong?

Her problem was a familiar one: "The boss doesn't appreciate me."
How did Zoe respond to her problem?

She avoided her boss!

Do you think that was a good tactic for achieving her goal of being promoted to VP? (She was ignoring her primary target market!)

Think Truth or Consequences

Emotionally, I could understand why Zoe wanted to sit far away from her boss at meetings and avoid one-on-ones. But her behavior was career sabotage. It was completely counterproductive to her goal of becoming a corporate VP.

Zoe had established a distant, formal relationship with her boss. Things were so bad by the time we started working together that she was communicating with him primarily through e-mail and memos and as infrequently as possible.

In her performance evaluations, Zoe's boss gave her high marks in many areas but consistently low marks in leadership and communications skills. Her boss told her that she needed to play a stronger role in initiating projects, selling them to management, and increasing her visibility in the firm.

Of course, Zoe felt that she had done all these things, often more than colleagues who had been promoted. After all, she had 47 people reporting to her. But, her boss didn't perceive her as being a leader or having a high enough profile to be a VP.

Perception Is Everything

The business world, like most places, operates on *perceptions*.

It really didn't matter that Zoe supervised a larger group than her colleagues had. She was viewed as a weak brand and not a vice president brand. And, in most companies, if your boss doesn't nominate you for VP, you will not have those two letters appearing after your name no matter how good you are.

So, if this happens to you, the choice is clear: You must either change your boss's perceptions of you or find a new boss somewhere else.

Zoe was stuck in an outdated junior image.

Our task was to develop a self-brand action plan that would change people's perceptions so that Zoe would be seen as the leader she is. She needed to improve her communication and presentation skills and dramatically increase her visibility inside and outside the firm.

Take Action for a New Reaction

Above all, Zoe needed to stop avoiding her boss. She had to emotionally engage him in what she could do.

To begin that process, she had to build rapport with her boss by meeting with him, making eye contact, and interacting in a more relaxed manner.

Rather than approach him as the "boss" or the "enemy," Zoe had to approach him as a trusted confidant (even as a friend). She needed to replace her negative self-talk with a positive mantra ("My boss is my ally").

Zoe had to approach him as if he were the way she wanted him to be. Often, if we treat people in a certain way, they start behaving to match. If that didn't work, her plan B was to launch a job search.

Improve What You Can

Zoe also worked on slowing down her rapid-fire speech. She spoke so fast that I often had to replay her voice-mail messages to decipher them!

One of the first things she did was join Toastmasters. After she gained some experience with that group, she offered to give a talk at a local university in order to develop more confidence in her presentation skills.

Little by little, Zoe started getting a different response from her boss and others at the firm as she became a better communicator. She also increased her visibility within the company by volunteering to lead an important strategic initiative.

When Zoe's boss selected her to represent him at an important company-wide meeting in Europe, we knew she had turned the corner. (And Zoe did get her happy ending. She made VP, and the company even added a new group to her department.)

VIEW COMPANY EXECS AS A MARKET

Colleagues and senior executives at your company are important target markets.

Henry, a financial services exec, is a master at developing formidable internal networks. The speed with which he put a network in place at his new firm was nothing short of "I came, I saw, I conquered."

Here's how he did it. When he started his new job, he saw an opportunity to put together innovative client events and programs directed at key client segments.

Rather than just put together programs that broke new ground with the client market, Henry also chose topics that were appealing to his consumer target and earmarked themes that appealed to key internal executives (his target market).

For example, the company's chief financial officer was involved in charitable groups that dealt with children and education. Henry put together a client event on America's education crisis, something of concern to the parent market segment his financial company was targeting. He invited a nationally recognized speaker on the topic and asked the CFO to introduce the speaker. Henry also put together a women's event with a well-known media figure and asked the firm's female executive vice president to make the introductions.

All the client events were successful with their target markets, and they were also a big coup for Henry. In short order, he had strong bonds with executives at all levels and in all parts of the company.

Looking at colleagues as a target market is important for anyone. You may not be able to apply Henry's maneuvers, but there are many opportunities at most companies to volunteer for projects that will put you in touch with a wider group of colleagues. Volunteer. Build relationships. It's much easier to be promoted with the support of other company executives.

OFFER SOMETHING COMPETITORS DON'T

Whatever your target market, you'll want to have a self-brand strategy that provides a compelling value proposition, a reason to choose you over your competitors.

One client, Kat, had a long career in video production and wanted to start her own business. The problem was that the video production category was crowded.

So we focused on a narrow segment of the market where she had special expertise, training videos and CD-ROMs for cosmetics companies. But there were some entrenched competitors here as well. When we started drawing up her strategy and value proposition for her target audience, we came up with a better idea.

Kat had some special attributes that set her apart and formed the core of our strategy.

She was a woman (and could provide a woman's touch) in the video production business, which was dominated by men.

She had a long history of producing high-end videos for top cosmetics brands. She knew how to get the lighting, makeup, and staging for top production values.

She also had a hidden asset. Before becoming a video producer, she had been a television morning show host in affiliate markets.

Bingo! We had our strategy: strong on both sides of the camera.

Defining her business proposition this way dramatically improved the power of her concept compared to those of her competitors. The value to clients was high-end know-how, whether they were preparing a video for their business or a media push that required someone to do a great job looking good in the public eye. It was a different idea, and one that resonated with her target audience.

Kat was able to tie together her assets: her strong client contacts, experience with some of the world's top cosmetics brands, experience as a television host, and a woman's touch to offer clients a clear value proposition.

Whether you are an executive or an entrepreneur like Kat, you need to have a value proposition that sets you apart from competitors. One way to test your value proposition is to draw a perceptual map like the one outlined in the following brainstormer. It will give you a graphic picture of your positioning strategy in relation to your competitors.

DON'T NEGLECT THE "L FACTOR"

Whether we like it or not, business is a popularity contest.

Likeability is the one thing all target markets must perceive in a brand, whether it is a product or a person.

That's why marketers develop a *brand personality* for a product or a company. Marketers also measure brand likeability. A new ad campaign, association with a celebrity, or alliance with another brand dramatically influences a brand's likeability.

‹‹ BRAINSTORMER ››

Creating a Perceptual Matrix

You'll need a piece of graph paper for graphing yourself or your company and key competitors on two key attributes that are critical to your positioning strategy. What's important is your idea of the perceptions a target market has about you or the others on these attributes.

First, draw a horizontal line through the middle of the paper to create a horizontal axis. In Kat's case, we used the attribute High-End Video Production Expertise, with the far left representing weakness and the far right representing strength.

Second, select another attribute to measure along the vertical axis. For Kat, we used On-Camera Experience, with the bottom representing no experience and the top representing strong experience.

Third, plot yourself and your competitors on the graph, locating the position that represents your relative strengths on the two key attributes you have selected.

Fourth, draw a line from your position to the upper right corner of the grid (the optimum position). This is your strategic path.

Unlike a product, you don't need to manufacture a brand personality. But always remember that personality is an important differentiator for a brand. You'll find the road to success much easier if you are perceived as likeable. Especially in markets like today's where there is a lot of choice, having a likeable personality can spell the difference between success and failure. Here are five general principles you can use to influence likeability:

1. *The Attractiveness Principle:* We have already discussed the importance of looks and packaging in self-branding. Attractiveness influences that all-important first impression. It has a halo effect and leads to a lot of positive assumptions.

2. *The Similarity Principle:* Finding common ground or relevance is a good networking tool, and it also influences likeability. We like people who are similar to us in some way, whether it is in personality, lifestyle, political beliefs, or an old school tie.

3. *The Empathy Principle:* The best way to get someone to like you is to like them. Put the focus on others. Empathize with them, and they will like you.

4. *The Familiarity Principle:* We like people with whom we are familiar and have contact, whether it's through personal contact or the media or by reputation. That's why visibility is important for people and brands.

5. *The Authenticity Principle:* Authenticity may be the cardinal rule of branding. You have to be yourself, not try to be someone else or fulfill other people's expectations and values.

Tom Hanks ranks high on most people's likeability meter.

What makes him so likeable?

Hanks is nice-looking, so he fulfills the Attractiveness Principle. But he's not too attractive, so he also taps into the Similarity Principle. Both his public and movie personae suggest that he is someone we could relate to, who treats others well, satisfying the Empathy Principle.

Hanks also fulfills the Familiarity Principle. Movies have made him famous and familiar. Many celebrities share their stories, experiences,

They say best men are moulded out of faults.
And, for the most, become much more the better
for being a little bad.

William Shakespeare
Measure for Measure **(V, 1)**

and values through the media. Fans feel that they know the celebrity and often become emotionally involved in that person's life.

Above all, Hanks seems to be a regular guy. He seems open and unaffected, which fulfills the Authenticity Principle. He appears to be comfortable in his own skin. He seems like someone you could get to know and someone you would want to be. In a word, Hanks is likeable.

‹‹ IN A NUTSHELL ››

The tenth secret of self-brands:

Think in terms of markets.

Determine what the market wants

and what you can do to appeal to the market

in a way no one else can.

BECOME A
LITTLE BIT FAMOUS

> *Have more than thou showest.*
> *Speak less than thou knowest.*
>
> **William Shakespeare**
> *King Lear* (I, 1)

Most of us have low wattage on the visibility spectrum. We are unknown outside of a small network of friends and professional contacts. We are not boldface names.

But visibility and its companion, fame, are things you should think about. We're talking here of fame on *some* level—famous in your industry, famous in your company, famous in your division, famous in your hospital, famous in your school, famous in your neighborhood. And we're talking here of being famous for *something*—an idea, a belief system, a point of view, a major achievement, an area of excellence.

You can build visibility for yourself in a subtle or heavy-handed, tasteful or obnoxious, outdated or up-to-date manner, but if you don't participate, you will be left behind.

It is impossible to become a brand without visibility. Marketers want visibility for their brands because visibility builds *mindshare*.

Mindshare brings big rewards. You can get a higher price for your services. People will seek you out. You will attract people to your ideas.

> MINDSHARE: Awareness of your brand versus those of competitors in the target market. High mindshare for your brand means sales leadership and pricing power.

More opportunities will be offered to you. And it will be easy to gain more visibility.

Of course, it is easy to scoff at the fame game as phony.

But the concept of visibility is part and parcel of our culture. It's not just the media machine that thrives on it.

Visibility is behind every product, every company, every nonprofit institution, every movement, and every person who achieves great things. Yes, visibility helps make the world go 'round.

BECOME TOP OF MIND

Despite things we've been told, like "talent wins out," the reality is more that "visibility wins out."

Talent and ability are important, but visibility alone may explain the difference between a professional who is in demand and earns a large salary and another professional who is just getting by. The truth is that people who have a reputation outside the company's walls have more value.

> *I'll note you in my book of memory.*
>
> **William Shakespeare**
> *King Lear* (II, 1)

One key measure of mindshare is *top of mind (TOM) awareness.* Market researchers ask questions such as, "When you think of category X, which brand comes to mind first?" Being top of mind, or the first brand mentioned by the target market, is a powerful advantage. It translates into sales leadership and gives you pricing power over your competitors.

It's the same with people. If you're visible and top of mind in your industry, people will make a lot of favorable assumptions about you. Fame tilts the playing field dramatically in your favor.

People assume that TOM performers are the top performers in their fields. If you are perceived as top of mind, you will be paid more, and more opportunities will come your way. You'll have what we in branding call *mindshare momentum*. Being the dominant, better-known brand in a category gives you strategic control.

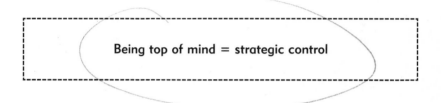

Being top of mind = strategic control

Why is being top of mind so rewarding?

People like things that are familiar and in the spotlight. This is true even if they aren't clear on why something is so well known. And people assume famous things are much better than things they have never heard of. Otherwise, why would they be famous?

For example, out of millions of paintings in the world, only a handful are well known everywhere.

The Mona Lisa tops that list. The Mona Lisa is number one in TOM awareness in the category of paintings.

Crowds flock to see the Mona Lisa every day. This painting is the only one to have a gallery of its own at the Louvre. It was given a leading role in best-selling books centuries after its time.

Is the Mona Lisa really the best painting in the world?

Who knows? But because it is top of mind, it has achieved icon status. It is truly priceless.

STUDY THE BRANDING MODEL

Brand managers build visibility and mindshare for their brands with a variety of tools: advertising, PR, events, product placement, Internet promotions, and hordes of other creative activities that bring the brand and its target market together.

Brand managers think in terms of (and measure) the *reach and frequency* of a brand message: how many people in the target audience saw a particular message or promotion and how many times they saw it. As a self-brand, you should think in terms of having a clear message and repeating that message so that people remember it too.

Advertisers track *net effective reach*, the optimum number of times the target market needs to be exposed to a message. They even track *wearout*, which is what happens when key market segments have seen a particular ad campaign enough times that it has become worn out and overexposed.

RUB SHOULDERS WITH A CELEBRITY

The celebrity endorsement is a well-known standby in the advertising business.

Studies by ad agencies tell us why the celebrity touch is so powerful. It's not because consumers really think that the product will necessarily be better but because they notice and pay attention to more of the sales message and are more likely to buy a product when a celebrity is behind it. Look at how Paul Newman sells spaghetti sauce. The "copy the stars" syndrome is also at work here. We have a need to model ourselves on heroes and superstars. We give them mythic stature and want to emulate their style.

The touch of a highly visible celebrity can jump-start demand for a product, company, or event. Adidas recently partnered with designer Stella McCartney to add sizzle to its shoe line. Certainly her designs were a breath of fresh air for a brand that had become lackluster, but the celebrity wattage of her name helped a lot, too. Now, it's hard to find Adidas shoes in stock.

Even being associated with a celebrity in some way will give you an enormous boost in visibility. When Kevin Federline married Britney Spears and Guy Ritchie married Madonna, it placed them front and center in the news and raised their position in the celebrity spectrum. Pairing up increased the star power of Catherine Zeta-Jones and Michael Douglas and Demi Moore and Ashton Kutcher. You can even get a halo effect just by displaying a picture of yourself together with a "celebrity" in your office or home. Notice the interest in photo ops with the mayor, or the company chief executive, or a celeb at a corporate outing.

Event planners seek out highly visible people to draw big crowds to corporate and civic events. Endorsement from a well-known person can move an unknown product or company into the big leagues. Former president Bill Clinton's endorsement of the South Beach Diet on a talk show boosted sales of the book almost overnight.

In summary, visibility gives you the following benefits:

> Credibility
> Awareness
> Differentiation
> Higher pay
> More visibility
> Awards of distinction
> Career opportunities

TAKE THE HOLLYWOOD ROAD

High visibility is often the strategy of choice for celebrities, television personalities, and sports stars when the worth of their personal brands depends on megavisibility. Sometimes visibility is the only strategy for a celebrity (for example, Paris Hilton).

Celebrity-making involves positioning, image development, packaging, story line, marketing messages, and PR, all aimed toward building and extending a person's shelf life, just as in brand development. *High Visibility*, by Irving Rein, Philip Kotler, and Martin Stoller, is a great book to read if you want to learn more about how the entertainment and sports worlds use visibility to create stars.

With celebrities, it's easy to tell who the stars are and who is at the red-hot center. You can look up each person's Q Score, Marketing Evaluations' ranking of celebrities in terms of their fame and popularity quotient, at http://www.qscores.com.

A high Q Score translates into getting tens of millions of dollars for the star role in a hot new movie. Advertisers want you for product endorsements. Publishers are eager to snag your new book. And fame opens up a list of opportunities that is long and growing longer as line extensions break new ground.

THE HOLLYWOOD MODEL

Talent + Packaging + PR = Star

Celebrities (and their agents) are constantly on the lookout for opportunities to gain visibility that would benefit their brands. You too should always keep your eyes open for ways to increase your visibility that are compatible with your self-brand and your profession. Below is a brainstormer to gauge your version of a Q Score, the G Score.

OPT FOR BUSINESS VISIBILITY

It used to be that businesspeople shunned visibility, but that was before the days of the celebrity CEO. Selection of a brand CEO can drive up a company's stock.

Likewise, the troubles of a celebrity chief can drive down a company's stock, as happened when ex-chiefs Dennis Kozlowski and Bernie Ebbers did the perp walk. Now, in the new world of Sarbanes-Oxley, chief executives are also tuned into the risks of being in the spotlight.

<< BRAINSTORMER >>

Gauging Your G Score

Gauge your visibility measure by Googling your name. Does your name come up? Are there many people with the same name, which diminishes your visibility? Is there an area where you could work on building your G Score?

Look at Martha Stewart. The damage was extreme because the company is essentially Stewart's self-brand. However, the company's stock regained positive momentum after Stewart and her company took charge of her self-brand again. After all, there is no sexier story than picking yourself up from a big fall and rebuilding your life for an against-all-odds second act.

Now, along with the celebrity CEO, there is the celebrity chef, celebrity entrepreneur, celebrity doctor, celebrity lawyer, and celebrity hairdresser, you name it. People running businesses of all sorts realize that visibility helps their businesses flourish.

CREATE BUZZ

Today, businesspeople have lots of avenues for visibility.

At the high end of the visibility spectrum, you can enhance your visibility through interviews on network and cable television or in consumer and business publications. You can give speeches at industry or outside events. You might choose to provide expert testimony. You could seek board seats at other companies or become involved with charities and philanthropic causes.

Like entertainment and sports celebrities, businesspeople are pursuing line extensions outside their areas of expertise as a way of expanding their brand footprint and perceived value. Buying a sports team, running for political office, and writing a book are all actions that pack a high visibility quotient.

Some businesspeople are even trespassing on celebrity turf by launching television shows, fueled by the success of Donald Trump and his reality show *The Apprentice*. After you've made piles of money, there's an attraction to becoming a "king of the hill, top of the heap" brand on television—the kind of fame and recognition we associate with television personalities. Publicity-driven CEOs such as Trump, Martha Stewart, and Richard Branson have turned PR into an art form. All are in a class by themselves, so adept are they at creating visibility and manipulating PR. Rappers are some of the best media and business crossover stars, adept at exploiting multiple media streams (think Sean "Diddy" Combs).

These days, no one is immune to the draw of visibility. In the past, academics were not known outside a small circle unless they published a best-selling book. Now, academics appear regularly on talk shows, speak around the country, and are quoted in the news along with being profiled in the alumni magazine.

BEGIN WITH LOW-VISIBILITY TACTICS

Most people aren't able to talk about their companies or their jobs to the outside media unless they are senior executives and have been authorized to do so. You probably can't use high-visibility tactics unless you are involved in an activity outside your job, such as chairing a fund-raising drive for a nonprofit or supporting a cause of personal interest to you.

But you can use a lot of low-visibility tactics to achieve more visibility within your company and your industry.

Start by taking a more active role, such as volunteering for cross-functional projects at work. Ask to participate in or lead corporate initiatives to which you can make a contribution. Besides learning something new, you will come into contact with executives outside your area in the company. Even something low-key, like setting up a monthly brown-bag lunch and inviting senior executives and outside vendors to speak, will help get you noticed outside your department.

Brush up your presentation skills so that you are an effective communicator both internally at meetings and externally with industry and other groups. As you become better at speaking and communicating, more opportunities will come your way.

Look for ways to make your talks special or set up a dramatic introduction for someone else. Think about how you enter a meeting. Don't ever rush in. Enter slowly, and if you are in a company where you can pull it off, grandly. I'll never forget my college experience of watching Margaret Mead enter the auditorium from the back of the room and walk down the aisle with an enormous walking stick. What a grand entrance!

When you talk about your ideas and proposals, use the branding techniques discussed earlier, such as naming your ideas to make them big ideas and coining words and expressions. Write an article for the company newsletter, or suggest a story about your department's new initiative. Don't make the story about you. Make it about the project, the idea, or the accomplishment. Glory will flow back to you, and you won't appear self-promoting.

The box below contains a list of high-visibility and low-visibility tactics used by businesspeople. It not only is a good review of what we've just discussed but may spur additional ideas of your own.

HIGH-VISIBILITY TACTICS VS. LOW-VISIBILITY TACTICS

HIGH-VISIBILITY TACTICS	LOW-VISIBILITY TACTICS
Expert on television	Project leader
Media interviews	High-level presentations
Book	Company projects
National media articles	Company newsletter
Charitable boards	Charitable activities
Corporate boards	Letters to the editor
Keynote speeches	Trade articles
Industry panels	Industry association activities
Website or blog	Proprietary reports
High-society events	White papers
Celebrity pal	Company Website

CHECK FOR ROOM IN THE CHANNEL

In seeking visibility, one thing you need to consider is whether there is "room in the channel," as they say in the business.

PR isn't a limitless thing. There is only so much room or coverage that can be absorbed by any one topic (with some notable exceptions, such as a juicy scandal).

As a rule, only a certain number of people can dominate each arena. Only a certain number of new faces can be highlighted each year.

Look at a major American event that is filled with high-visibility celebrities, such as the Academy Awards. The media focuses on the winners in the big categories, but after that, visibility reaches just those celebrities who wore a fabulous (or awful) dress or say something especially provocative (or incoherent) on stage. The channel simply doesn't have enough room to give visibility to every important person at the event.

Likewise, it's harder to find room in the channel in a geographic market like New York City, which is already crowded with top talent in every field. It will be much more difficult to break out unless you come up with something very special.

FIND AN ARENA YOU CAN DOMINATE

Look for an arena that is not already too crowded with others who staked out their spots before you. The first places to look are your job and your field. Then look at outside areas—cultural or political organizations or a cause that you are passionate about. Best of all, create a new cause or business idea to champion.

Every field produces celebrities: people who act as standard bearers. These people are the leaders who are active at industry events and are quoted on industry issues or on their specialty areas. Or they fill the role of expert, pundit, or contrarian. Every institution has a need for people to fill various archetypal roles. Some even become icons.

Think about where there might be room in the channel for you. Is it time for a changing of the guard? Are there issues in your field that are not well represented or even discussed? How can you get to know some of the influential people in the various arenas that interest you? Which ones would benefit most from your contribution?

STRATEGIZE YOUR BREAKOUT STORY

Think strategically about your *breakout story*, the first story that launches you in the media. It is your most important story, since it will position you in the minds of others and have lasting consequences.

Another thing to think about is whether your field is mediagenic. Some industries are inherently more high interest than others. It's much easier to generate visibility if you are in a high-profile business area such as finance, technology, media and entertainment, pharmaceuticals, and others that are of constant interest to the public.

If you work for a coal company, you will have trouble getting visibility for yourself and your company. You will have to generate visibility outside of your industry or have business insights with universal appeal.

Harvey Mackay ran an envelope company, a business that does not usually generate much interest. Mackay won megavisibility through his first business book, *Swim with the Sharks*. The PR on the book and his business insights (and humor) catapulted Mackay into the big time as a business leader and philosopher on winning in business. And he followed up his first success with other best-selling business books.

TOOT YOUR OWN HORN (GRACEFULLY)

If you hope to succeed at visibility, you need to control how you are perceived. Whether it's becoming better known in a small pond (your company) or a big pond (your industry) or the ocean (nationally), it's smart to package your message. You need to package it with a good name and sound bite so that it will break through, but you must also package it so that you don't appear to be promoting yourself.

> *The better part of valor is discretion.*
>
> **William Shakespeare**
> *Henry IV, Part One* **(V, 4)**

Here are the most important guidelines for promoting yourself effectively while avoiding the appearance of self-promotion:

> ❯ *Use a narrative or story format:* Presenting your accomplishments or ideas through dialogue and building suspense gets people involved in the story because it doesn't seem to be about you but about what happened. (Read Peggy Klaus's book *Brag!* for ideas on how to do this.)

> ❯ *Quote other people:* As they say, the best advertising is word of mouth. When another person sings your praises, it's the opinion of a third party, not your own judgment. ("I was really surprised when client Joe called to say . . .")

> ❯ *Put the spotlight elsewhere:* Don't focus on yourself. Put the spotlight on your new initiative or the company. Always make it about something larger than yourself.

> ❯ *Bring the audience into the story:* When you bring your audience into the story, it won't just be about you. ("I wish you could have been there when . . .")

LEAVE A ROLE FOR LADY LUCK

While I believe that you create your own luck, that doesn't mean people don't add a dollop of luck to their stories. They attribute their success to luck because the story goes over much better that way than telling people the truth. Namely, that you have been working 24/7 on building your career.

I appreciate this below

> **Luck is the big white lie in most success stories.**

Luck is a key element in most stories of achievement. Luck makes people look like they did not plan their success or use PR or managers to promote themselves. Many people think it is somehow wrong to go after success.

The reality in almost every case is the opposite. Almost no one achieves great things or becomes a well-known self-brand without wanting it and working very hard to achieve it. Strategy and planning have more to do with achieving success than luck does.

People who achieve great things work smart in order to achieve their goals, often with the help of coaches, branding experts, and PR specialists. But most people would rather not hear about all that planning and hard work.

So if you say, "Gee, I just got lucky. They needed an architect to design the new arts center, and I guess I was in the right place at the right time," or, "I didn't mean for this to happen," people will respond in a positive way.

MASTER THE MEDIA

Today, more than 70 percent of news comes from PR sources. The media have a tremendous need for content, and, as a person who is interested in promoting your self-brand, you'll need to know how to give them good content that will benefit you and your organization.

Never make a media interview about you.

Make the interview about what you did or your point of view, not about you personally. By making the project, the new product, or the new initiative the focus of the interview, you will not be the center of attention, but attention will come to you.

> **Remember, your job is to stay on message.**
>
> **The reporter's job is to get you to say something off message.**

Prepare a media talking points memo in advance of big meetings and certainly before a media interview. Include the most likely questions and role-play your answers beforehand. Think of stories, anecdotes, and sound bites ahead of time. Is there a way to present elements of your story as news?

It is also smart to be prepared with at least one point of view that's different from the prevailing view if you want maximum media coverage.

If a question is offtrack, bring the reporter back to the message you want to give. Reporters are looking for a good story. A good story is when you say something controversial. It's your job to stay in control of the message, no matter what question you are asked.

GUARD YOUR REPUTATION

People at the top of their game often develop a false sense of invulnerability.

In fact, they are more vulnerable.

You should realize that you will be living in a fishbowl when you become a boldface name.

> *There's daggers in men's smiles.*
>
> **William Shakespeare**
> *Macbeth* (II, 3)

People will scrutinize your words and actions more closely than when you were not so well known. Some will be looking for mistakes or questionable activities. Jealous competitors may try to take potshots at you.

And as much as the media likes to build people up, it also likes to take people down. The story of Ms. Big's fall from grace sells. As does the juicy scandal that Mr. Big got caught up in. When something like this happens, it gives people the feeling of schadenfreude, or delight in the misfortunes of others.

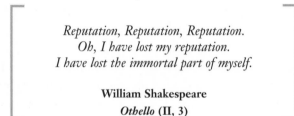

Reputation, Reputation, Reputation.
Oh, I have lost my reputation.
I have lost the immortal part of myself.

William Shakespeare
Othello **(II, 3)**

And you have a lot to lose. The name you spent a lifetime building can be tarnished or even torn down very quickly. Studies show that it takes a lot of promotion of good acts to build a reputation, yet just a little promotion of one bad act to tarnish it.

That's why it's wise to adopt the mind-set that there are no secrets and that people will find out everything. If you're presented with the chance to be involved in something that would truly destroy your reputation if it were known, let that opportunity pass you by. More than losing possessions, losing your reputation will severely damage your self-brand identity.

If you are about to get caught in a PR nightmare, try to take control of the story. The old PR saying goes, "Tell them everything and tell them first."

Reputations take a long time to build, but a short time to destroy.

If the news gets out in front of you, there are still things you can do. Look at how Jack Welch handled the bad publicity about his rich retirement package from GE. Rather than let the "greedy" label stick, he gave back some of the excessive retirement perks. A year later, he came out with a book, *Winning*, to get his brand back in the mindspace he wants to own. Welch is giving the profits from the book to charity, a fact he spells out at the bottom of the book's dedication page. This is a generous thing to do, but also a smart thing if he wants to change misperceptions about being greedy.

Of course, sometimes bad news stories can have a silver lining. Hillary Clinton's image improved after the Monica Lewinsky scandal. People saw her in a more sympathetic light. Likewise, Martha Stewart's travails and prison stint helped humanize her. And Paris Hilton's appeal only increased after her sex tape made its way into the consumer media.

Managing your reputation is a skill you must master if you intend to build your self-brand, whether you're well known in a national or international arena or a little bit famous in your company or community.

But build your reputation and visibility with finesse. You want to be known for something, but not for being a self-promoter.

The key to doing self-promotion well is to do it without looking like you are doing it.

‹‹ IN A NUTSHELL ››

The eleventh secret of self-brands:

Make yourself a little bit famous.

Find an arena you can dominate

and build a self-brand identity.

DEVELOP AN ACTION PLAN THAT GETS YOU ALL THE WAY FROM A TO Z

> *Action is eloquence.*
>
> **William Shakespeare**
> *Coriolanus* (III, 2)

Defining a great self-brand strategy is one thing. Making your strategy a reality is another.

You may have a great strategy and a focused visual and verbal identity, but you'll never get anywhere until you pay off your brand promise with an action plan. Without a tactical plan, your success is left to chance.

Executing a self-brand strategy requires persistence and action. Brand managers use a marketing plan to tie it all together, and you should, too.

COMMIT TO ACTION

The hardest part of a big endeavor is getting started. You must, of course, start.

Most people become so daunted by the task of developing a personal branding plan that they procrastinate. The key is to get started with a short plan (aim for five pages). Lay on one tactic after another that will help you reach your goal.

All things are ready if our minds be so.

William Shakespeare
King Henry V (IV, 3)

Things will add up. Often, just implementing one action item leads to another item. (Even if it's the wrong one, you will be learning. And learning leads to the next step.)

WRITE DOWN TACTICS

Writing the action plan is important because it forces you to tie your strategy to tactics and to set specific goals and target dates.

A self-brand action plan includes the following:

> *Goals:* Lay out the path you plan to take by setting two or three concrete goals for yourself.

> *SWOT analysis:* Review your strengths and weaknesses and the opportunities and threats you see in the marketplace. Include an analysis of your key competitors.

> *Target markets:* List your primary and secondary target markets.

> *Self-brand strategy:* Define your self-brand strategy, the brand positioning that sets you apart from competitors and offers a benefit to your target market. Make it short and punchy, like a mantra. (Reread chapter 4 and the 10 strategies outlined there if you need to refresh your memory.) Follow your strategy statement with 3–5 proof points (reasons to believe your strategic positioning).

> *Time frame:* Set a time frame to check your progress against.

> *Tactics:* Outline a series of specific marketing and professional activities that will help you reach your goals. Include the amount of time scheduled for each tactic and the likely results.

> *Measurement:* Measure the success of your action plan by noting your progress toward achieving your concrete goals.

Use the next brainstormer to get started on your action plan.

‹‹ BRAINSTORMER ››

Making a Plan

If you have already done the brainstormers in the other chapters, you're halfway there.

Pull together the goals from the brainstormer in chapter 1, the SWOT and competitive analyses you did in chapter 2, and the strategy statement from chapter 4 and combine them in one document, your self-brand action plan.

Then, list specific things you can do to achieve your goals and implement your self-brand strategy.

STAY RELEVANT

A self-brand marketing plan is not carved in stone.

Situations change. You change.

Sometimes it's a mixture of self-imposed change and market-induced change.

Change always creates new challenges and opportunities. It requires new strategies and tactics. So, look at your action plan periodically to make sure that your strategy and tactics are right for the current marketplace. Fortunately, people are more adaptable and can change tactics or even strategies more easily than most companies and products can.

Look at Howard Dean. Dean began as a doctor, entered politics, and became governor of Vermont. He entered the primary race for president of the United States, built a lot of momentum, and then had a sudden reversal of fortune. He was thought to be dead politically until he resurrected himself as chairman of the Democratic National Committee.

MOVE THE PLOT

If you take over a new job, the first 100 days are the most important. Notice how the media follows the first 100 days in office of a new president. Your behavior and actions when you start a new job will be scrutinized and have a strong impact on how you are perceived over the long haul.

Remember the importance of first impressions. Come out of the gate running with an action plan. Create a vision and a plot for your team to follow and rally around. And keep the plot moving along in the direction you want.

Your self-brand is constantly changing whether you do anything or not. If you don't keep a successful narrative going, the story line could get away from you, and you will be regarded as yesterday's sensation.

Take Luke. Because of his hard work and the successful team projects that he led, he rose quickly at an industrial company. He was known as a leader who understood what was going on in the manufacturing plants.

After being at the company for a number of years, Luke grew a little bit complacent and wasn't working as hard as he had in the past.

Then he got a new boss who didn't know about his past deeds. And Luke didn't have any recent accomplishments that might have kept his leadership alive in the corporate memory.

Six months later, Luke was given a tough job review. All of a sudden, his star, which had been on the rise for so long, was flickering out.

Was the new boss's assessment fair? Probably not.

Did the new boss have his own agenda? Probably.

But the greatest learning experiences often come from bad bosses.

The less-than-stellar review certainly woke Luke up to the fact that he wasn't bulletproof.

DISCARD DOUBTS

Self-confidence usually takes a beating in a situation like Luke's. His certainly did.

He started second-guessing himself and doubting his abilities. He circled the wagons and shut himself off in his office. And that led to more depression and inaction.

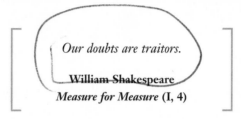

Our doubts are traitors.

William Shakespeare
Measure for Measure (I, 4)

Self-confidence or the perception of self-confidence is a big career booster. And the lack of it is a career buster. To be a successful self-brand, you have to protect your self-confidence. Otherwise, when you feel you are under attack, even if you were once as supremely self-confident as Luke, you will come across like a wimp. For a while, Luke was almost a basket case.

He needed to start believing in himself again and put the experience in perspective. The new boss's bad review was just one person's opinion in a long career of achievement.

Luke needed to protect himself from the impact of his boss's negative perception by focusing on what he knew to be true about himself and by taking action.

FIGHT BACK

Many people get bogged down in what the boss did or didn't do.

It is impossible to control what other people do and think. But you can always control your reaction and what you are going to do.

Luke initiated an action plan with a two-pronged offensive. One group of tactics addressed his boss's concerns about his performance. The other group of tactics supported a major job search.

> *We have seen better days.*
>
> **William Shakespeare**
> *Timon of Athens* **(IV, 2)**

After the negative review, Luke wrote his boss a long, positive memo about his performance evaluation. In it, he detailed bullet point by bullet point the actions he was taking to address each performance item. He also met with human resources to create a record of his contention that, even though he felt the performance evaluation was unduly harsh, he was committed to turning things around.

> **You can't always control a negative situation.**
>
> **But you can control how you respond to it.**

Luke took these steps even though he suspected that the new boss had given him the unfavorable evaluation because he wanted to bring his own person in to fill Luke's position.

DO A SELF-AUDIT

Sure, Luke had made some mistakes. Maybe he hadn't stayed current and on top of new trends. For one thing, many of his company's competitors were outsourcing or locating new plants in Asia. Luke and others at his company were behind on this trend, so now competitors had a pricing advantage. But since Luke was in trouble (and the corporate politicians could sense it), he got more than his share of the blame.

Perhaps Luke had become too reactive, building his workday activities around the many e-mail and BlackBerry messages he got each day. He realized that he wasn't bringing enough strategic vision and big-picture ideas to the business.

But he didn't really recognize the person described in his new boss's harsh evaluation. Nor was the boss very helpful when Luke approached him for direction on an important company issue.

Why did Luke take these steps with his boss and HR?

A job search takes time, and he needed to buy time in which to find something else. There was also the possibility (however unlikely) of turning things around with his new boss or locating another position in the firm. In any case, as long as Luke was working at the company, he had to try to build a positive relationship with his boss, a key target market.

CREATE A NEW BRAND POSITION

Of course, Luke felt set up. But once he accepted the unfairness of the situation, he was able to take charge. We did the SWOT analysis and developed a strategy and an action plan. Luke started setting his own agenda, rather than leaving it to his boss.

Luke's action plan got him to refocus on what had made him great in the first place. He had built his brand on his hands-on, nurturing style of leadership. His roots were in operations, and he knew how to build teams within the organization to get things done. He had been a master of managing from the bottom up and sideways across the organization.

The key thing Luke needed to do was change perceptions—of his boss, other key executives, even the rank and file in the field. He knew his boss was raising the issue with senior management of whether Luke was the right leader for today's highly competitive, global marketplace. He needed to create a different impression. He needed to show that he was able to lead in innovation and manufacturing with pricing power over his competitors.

Initially, Luke concentrated on actions that would lead to positive outcomes. His relationship with field operations had always been a source of business inspiration and had given him a performance edge. Luke started visiting the manufacturing plants and field offices more frequently.

He also worked on some small projects that allowed him to score some early victories. He pressed forward on a new product that did much better than expected in the marketplace. And he put together his own team to explore outsourcing and manufacturing outside the United States.

VOLUNTEER FOR THE IMPOSSIBLE

Luke also volunteered to lead the company's big initiative to increase competitiveness by taking a more global approach to manufacturing and other functions where it made sense. No one else wanted to take it on (at least in the lead role). It was a difficult project with a lot of moving parts. In a way, Luke had nothing more to lose but a lot to gain.

The project increased his visibility among many executives with whom he normally didn't come into contact, including the president. He updated his boss frequently on the project's progress, so that the boss would have no reason for complaint. The global initiative also gave Luke hands-on knowledge of and experience with China, India, and other low-cost manufacturing and outsourcing centers his company was exploring. Luke found that his strong interpersonal and team-building skills served him well on the new global playing field. He made important contacts and was building relationships that would be valuable to his company in the future. (Of course, Luke realized that the new initiative made him infinitely more attractive as a job prospect, if it came to that.)

By focusing on his strengths (his relationship with operations employees and his ability to lead cross-functional team projects), Luke also drew attention to the weaknesses of his new boss, who was numbers driven and a poor people person.

> **When you have a competitor or a detractor with a weakness, emphasize your strength in the same area.**

It came about naturally in Luke's case, but it's a smart strategy to use with any competitor: Look at your competition's weaknesses, and position a weakness against a key strength of yours. Emphasize where you are strong and they are weak. Luke's strength with people and with organizing global teams emphasized the boss's lack of people skills.

CARRY A BRAG BOOK

The more Luke took charge of his life, the less victimized he felt and the more success he had in his job hunt and at his company.

As a way of marketing himself effectively, Luke put together a brag book so that he had all his successful initiatives at his fingertips. It was a nice presentation folder that contained the following self-brand marketing pieces:

> Letters of recognition

> Key initiatives, organized in a case study format (challenge, action, results), like a new business pitch

> Awards for achievement

> Luke's letters in recognition of others

> Testimonials and references

Luke polished up his elevator speech and put together a résumé that sold his accomplishments as a dynamic leader and innovator in his industry, highlighting his leadership of the firm's globalization initiative.

In interviews, Luke had a strong self-presentation and a leave-behind (the brag book). He developed interesting narratives on each of his key projects, linking together his accomplishments and portraying himself as a "man of the people," and a "global manufacturing leader." He did his homework on each company so that the meeting would be a conversation, not a one-way question-and-answer session.

CREATE SIGNATURE SUCCESSES

Luke didn't waste much energy on unproductive activities like complaining about his new boss. He focused on his strengths and on activities that would lead to positive outcomes—*signature successes* that would put him on the radar screens of senior executives and on a better track with his new boss, or that would help him locate a desirable job at another company.

Here are some of the tactics in his action plan and measurement goals:

> Volunteer for a major company initiative to demonstrate leadership, to build stronger ties throughout the company, and to become an expert in Asian manufacturing and outsourcing. *Measurement:* Achieve project goals set by company president.

> Send a memo about the performance review to the boss and to HR, outlining specific actions for addressing critical areas.

Measurement: Send a monthly memo to the boss and to HR and meet quarterly with both to evaluate progress.

> Get in better touch with operations by planning two to three trips a month and scheduling regular times to talk to operations management. *Measurement:* Trips scheduled and calls made each month.

> Revise résumé and develop compelling cover letter and brag book for job search. Customize the résumé and letter for each interview. *Measurement:* Set a target date for document completion.

> Develop a short list of companies to explore and a networking list of contacts. *Measurement:* Ten discussions or meetings per month, with a company, a recruiter, or a networking contact.

Luke's action plan kept him busy and focused on his goals.

The outcome in his case was interesting and totally unexpected.

About seven months after Luke completed his internal makeover and began his external job hunt, his boss got a new boss. And within six months, the boss who had been trying to push Luke out was sent packing.

But Luke probably won't be resting on his past accomplishments anytime soon. More than ever before, Luke realizes that being happy and powerful in your life requires action. You have to get out there and do it. You have to keep your narrative moving along so it is relevant and vital.

CREATE PERCEIVED VALUE

Whether you are an executive, a professional, or an entrepreneur, a self-brand action plan also helps you create a sense of value added—the X factor—that sets your self-brand and your business apart from the rest.

After all, the whole point of branding and the action plan is to help you prepare to win. You need to have both the sizzle and the steak to win in today's marketplace.

Let's look at a world that, until recently, was as far removed from Luke's world or the world of branding as you could get.

> *We should do when we would, for this "would" changes.*
>
> **William Shakespeare**
> *Hamlet* (IV, 8)

With the decline in the family farm and the difficulty experienced by small farming operations, farmers who want to remain viable have been forced to brand their enterprises in order to survive.

Take honey suppliers, for example. Because of global competition, American honey suppliers have had to compete with foreign suppliers whose costs are dramatically lower.

Selling honey in bulk as they had done in the past means losing money and dividing the farm into house lots. One solution is to add value through branding so as to justify their higher prices. Instead of generic honey, you now have local honeys such as Happy Valley Farms Organic Clover and Wildflower Honey, produced in small batches in rural Vermont.

In October 2004, the *New Yorker* did a feature story on MaryJane Butters, who's re-creating a mystique and lifestyle for the American farm much as Ralph Lauren did for American WASP culture.

Butters created a new category, American farm girl, in which she could be first. She created a brand and a special brand experience that catapulted her farm into the limelight.

Here are some of the items in her action plan:

> A Website that displays her farm products with whimsy and style

> Farm tours, stays, and events

> A magazine, *MaryJane*, on her farm-girl concept

> A book series on her farm concept

As Butters says, "People wanted to go to a farm, reconnect with that, see what a farm does, what a farm is. The U-Pick thing was a hit, the music, being outside in a beautiful setting, the hay bales in the field. Totally like Disneyland reinvented."

Butters is a farm girl who is a student of branding. As she says, "I branded myself so people would ask, 'Who is this MaryJane?'"

LEAD WITH YOUR STRONG SUIT

Always play to your strengths and your authenticity. It's easy to forget this maxim as we're offered different opportunities in life.

Take Julius. Julius was an entrepreneur who built a small but successful niche in financial services. After a few years, one of his clients offered to buy his business and put Julius in charge of the division at the company.

Julius was smart, creative, and visionary. He was decisive and made things happen. He was charismatic and a super salesman. And he was likeable.

Sounds like all the right traits to succeed in a large global company, right?

Wrong!

Sure, his intelligence, salesmanship, and creativity were valued at the company, but many of the strengths that made Julius a great entrepreneur were weaknesses in a large corporate environment.

Julius was used to making decisions himself, so he got frustrated with the bureaucracy. Sometimes he didn't go through channels. He rubbed managers the wrong way when he didn't solicit their help or win their buy-in. Sometimes he became angry and emotional in dealing with colleagues when he felt they weren't being cooperative.

Before long, Julius was no longer running the division—his baby, the business he had created from scratch. The company brought someone in over him. Julius was now number two.

REMEMBER WHAT MADE YOU GREAT

When I first met Julius, he was angry. He felt like a victim, even a failure. He was so upset that he wasn't going to work.

Interestingly, the company wanted Julius to come back either in the number two role or in another position. The company valued his intelligence and sales skills and even signed off on a coach.

Julius may have felt like a failure because he was no longer running his business, but the word "failure" hardly applied. He had created and sold a business for great profit at a young age. Not many people achieve that in a lifetime.

The key question Julius needed to answer was "Do you want to be an entrepreneur brand or a corporate executive brand?" He also needed to find out what he had to learn from this experience. What behaviors should he change or improve on so that they wouldn't haunt him the next time around?

DO A 360-DEGREE TURN

Just as brand managers do market research with key target markets, we did a SelfBrand Audit, confidential interviews with 10 people including senior executives, colleagues, direct reports, and family members. (People often tell me that they may have a bit of a difficult reputation at work, but they are completely different at home. Yet, when I talk to their spouses, they tell more or less the same story I hear at the office!)

Our goal in the audit was to gauge perceptions of Julius: who he was, what his strengths and weaknesses were, and what was different and even remarkable about him.

Branding is a game of perceptions. This is true whether the brand is for a company, a product, or a person. What you want to say and do are less important than what the market experiences of you. What are you doing that the target market loves? What are you doing that is tarnishing your brand and turning off your customers?

Target markets often have insights about you and how you bring meaning to the world that you can't see because you're too close to the brand. That's why marketers constantly keep in touch with their target markets through focus groups, one-on-one interviews, and larger surveys.

FOCUS ON STRENGTHS AND AUTHENTICITY

When we did the market research on Julius, we found the following key themes:

> Julius made a great first impression (likeable, smart, strong self-presentation) but tarnished the image by being overly emotional for a corporate environment.

> Julius was smart and creative and had an entrepreneurial flair, but follow-through in a corporate environment could be a problem.

> Julius was a super salesperson who developed strong client relationships, but he needed to translate those people skills to his interactions with colleagues at work. (In other words, he would fare better if he tried to woo colleagues as if they were clients.)

Like all of us, Julius had formidable strengths and weaknesses. Of course, he could transform himself so that he would perform well in a corporate environment, but should he?

In so many ways, Julius was a natural entrepreneur. He had the smarts, creativity, and drive to develop and incubate business ideas. He was interested in gaining financial rewards for himself and his investors.

(His concern about his earn-out at the company was another area that rankled the more traditional corporate execs at the firm.)

By focusing on his authenticity and his strengths, Julius was able to focus on the path that was right for him. He no longer had to accept the way he had been treated at the company either.

Rather than accept the corporate posts the company was offering him, Julius presented a proposal to the division president about creating the new position of intrapreneur. As an intrapreneur, Julius would be responsible for coming up with ideas for start-ups that would expand business with the company's existing customer base.

Julius also explored ideas for business start-ups outside the company and put together a business plan for the one with the most promise.

Now, Julius had a strategy and an action plan that played exactly to his strengths. With these, he was able to see good options for his future.

CREATE LINKS TO GET FROM A TO B TO C

One thing I have found in working with all types of clients is that practically anything is possible. This is true whether your goal is a promotion or a new job, getting the corner office or getting into the right school, rejoining the workforce after a long absence, or rebranding the family business.

Think of your goals. Brainstorm. Take baby steps first. Create a chain of links. What is one little thing you can do to get yourself moving in the direction of achieving your goal? What else can you do? Start building links on a chain to get yourself from one point to the next.

Apply the branding mind-set and the branding process.

If what you're doing isn't working, try something else. Branders change tactics all the time. Even if a tactic is working great for you now, at some point it won't work as well or will wear out. Like a brand manager, you will have to change and refresh the experience. Marketers refresh the brand experience all the time. They might try a new advertising campaign, a new promotion, a special event, new packaging, or a celebrity tie-in.

Our virtues lie in the interpretation of the time.

William Shakespeare
Coriolanus (IV, 7)

The best way to come up with a good idea is to think of a lot of ideas. You may not be able to use them all, but some will be worthwhile. Focus on the best ideas and see where they lead you. Try a different tactic and see where it takes you.

When things are going well and you're on a roll, that is the time to push for more. That is the time for bold actions and new projects. Ask for the big raise or the promotion. Seek out more visibility.

And, never forget, you're never really finished unless you drop out.

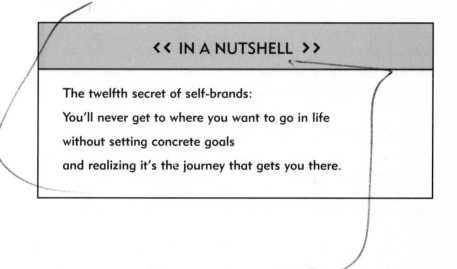

‹‹ IN A NUTSHELL ››

The twelfth secret of self-brands:

You'll never get to where you want to go in life

without setting concrete goals

and realizing it's the journey that gets you there.

‹‹ Afterword ››

Nothing is either good or bad,
but thinking makes it so.

William Shakespeare
Hamlet **(II, 2)**

Business success, like branding, is a game of perceptions.

If people think you are at the top of your game, you are. If people think you are a bit player, you will be one until you change their thinking.

When you are competing for something—whether to head up the company, the new business pitch, or the PTA—it doesn't matter who is "objectively" better for the job. What matters are the impressions in the minds of other people. Those perceptions about you control your destiny.

Self-branding is a way of thinking and doing to help you take back control of your destiny and create positive perceptions for the brand You. It isn't just about self-promotion (though that will be a result). Self-branding shows you how to maximize your assets in a way that will benefit both you and the company. You'll be able to perform better and be more effective by thinking strategically in terms of markets and needs. You'll harness soft power through "packaging" a compelling visual identity and verbal identity. You'll learn how to differentiate yourself so that you are relevant and memorable.

The world of brands is not static. Neither is yours. Branding is a way of thinking and responding to changing market conditions. When things are going well, that is the time to step up your branding programs and go for big gains in the marketplace (introducing new initiatives, seeking a big promotion, starting a new venture, and so on).

There is a tide in the affairs of men
which taken at the flood, leads on to fortune.

William Shakespeare
Julius Caesar **(IV, 3)**

good stuff

Markets can shift, too. They can even disappear completely, leaving you as relevant as the buggy whip. But branding gives you a method for repositioning, rebranding, and relaunching yourself and your business arena. You don't want to end up adrift in the tough business marketplace lamenting, "How could this have happened?" or "How can I be riffed? I've worked here for twenty years!"

You want to be able to smell change coming and focus your energies on analyzing the new marketplace and finding new ideas and options. You need to be opportunistic and develop tactics to get back in the game for a successful second act. And, whether it's a big pond or a small pond you're swimming in, you need to have a good understanding of your competition so that you can keep what you offer relevant as the market twists and turns, or as your company gets downsized or merged.

While I have presented a lot of guidelines for self-branding, there are no hard and fast "branding rules." You can break a branding principle and still be phenomenally successful. The branding highway is filled with brands that broke a guideline (or two or three) and were a hit anyway. It happens all the time. (Remember, branding is more an art than a science.)

> *Fair is foul. Foul is fair.*
>
> **William Shakespeare**
> *Macbeth* **(I, 1)**

Just as there are no concrete branding rules, there are no hard and fast business or life rules. Something that worked for someone else may work for you, but it may not. Something that was a career buster for one person may be the critical event leading to a wonderful opportunity for you.

Almost nothing is objectively "good" or "bad." It's our perception of whether it's good or bad that makes it good or bad.

Each of us is unique, with a brain, looks, strengths, and experiences that are powerful assets. Anyone you know, or have known; anything you have ever done or thought about can be an asset.

If you think something is an asset, it is. If you see it as a stepping-stone to your self-branding goal, it is. If you see it as a dead end, it is. We all have hundreds of assets and opportunities. But they are worthless unpless we recognize them as positive things and take action accordingly.

In business, as in life, success is much more likely if you feel positive about yourself and your experiences, and if you stay in the moment rather than hold onto past glories or the way things used to be.

But even more important to your success is cultivating positive perceptions in the minds of others about who you are and what you've done and what you can do. You need to attract people to your ideas and abilities. You need to have that "something more" so that people want you and no one else. Self-branding gives you strategies and guidelines for harnessing those outside perceptions and market dynamics so that you can make the most of your most important asset, You.

⟨⟨ About the Author ⟩⟩

From Madison Avenue to Wall Street to the halls of academe, Catherine Kaputa perfected her ability to market products, places, and companies. She first learned brand strategy from Al Ries and Jack Trout at Trout & Ries Advertising, and then led the award-winning "I ❤ NY" campaign at Wells, Rich, Greene. For over ten years she was SVP, Director of Advertising and Community Affairs at Citi Smith Barney, and she taught branding at New York University's Stern School of Business.

Yet Catherine has discovered that the most important application for branding is not for products, places, and companies—it's for individuals to define and own their career identity and create their success.

That's why Catherine launched SelfBrand LLC, a New York City-based personal branding company, and wrote the award-winning book, *You Are a Brand!: How Smart People Brand Themselves for Business Success* (paperback edition 2009, www.youareabrandbook.com). The original hardcover edition of the book, *U R a Brand!*, was winner of the Ben Franklin award for Best Career Book 2007, and a bronze IPPY award. Concerned about women's success in the workplace, Catherine wrote *The Female Brand: Using the Female Mindset to Succeed in Business* (2009, www.femalebrand.com).

Catherine is active as a speaker, workshop leader, and career coach at a wide range of corporations and organizations as part of talent development, sales training, corporate meetings, and diversity and women's initiatives. Her focus in self-branding is not on changing who you are but becoming who you can be—particularly important in today's competitive business climate. (To find out more about SelfBrand and Catherine's speaking programs and coaching, visit www.selfbrand.com.)

She has been featured on ABC, NBC, MSNBC, *The Wall Street Journal*, *The New York Times*, *USA Today*, Fortune.com, CNN/Money.com, and was a "Cool Friend" on TomPeters.com. Her speaking clients include PepsiCo, Microsoft, Intel, UBS, Boehringer Ingelheim, UST, and The Bank of New York Mellon.

Catherine has been a brand builder throughout her life—but the biggest branding leap was her first one when she switched from being a

Japanese art historian to becoming a branding expert. Catherine has a B.A. from Northwestern University, an M.A. from the University of Washington, and was a Ph.D. candidate at Harvard University. She also spent two years at Tokyo University on a Japanese Ministry of Education fellowship. Catherine blogs at www.artofbranding.com and lives in New York City with her husband and son.

Catherine would love to hear your self-branding stories and advice. Email her at catherinekaputa@gmail.com.

‹‹ Resources ››

Beckwith, Harry. *What Clients Love: A Field Guide to Growing Your Business*. New York: Warner Business Books, 2003.

Bridges, William. *Creating You & Co.: Learn to Think Like the CEO of Your Own Career*. Reading, MA: Addison-Wesley, 1997.

Cialdini, Robert B. *Influence, Science, and Practice*. Boston: Allyn and Bacon, 2001.

Corcoran, Barbara, with Bruce Littlefield. *If You Don't Have Big Breasts, Put Ribbons in Your Pigtails*. New York: Portfolio, 2003.

D'Alessandro, David F., Michele Owens, and Michael Owens. *Career Warfare: 10 Rules for Building a Successful Personal Brand and Fighting to Keep It*. New York: McGraw-Hill, 2003.

Ferrazzi, Keith, and Tahl Raz. *Never Eat Lunch Alone: And Other Secrets to Success One Relationship at a Time*. New York: Currency, 2005.

Frankel, Alex. *Word Craft: The Art of Turning Little Words into Big Business*. New York: Crown, 2004.

Friedman, Thomas L. *The World Is Flat: A Brief History of the Twenty-first Century*. New York: Farrar, Straus & Giroux, 2005.

Gerstner, Louis V., Jr. *Who Says Elephant's Can't Dance?* New York: HarperBusiness, 2003.

Gladwell, Malcolm. *The Tipping Point: How Little Things Can Make a Big Difference*. Boston: Little, Brown, 2000.

Gladwell, Malcolm. *Blink: The Power of Thinking Without Thinking*. Boston: Little, Brown, 2005.

Godin, Seth. *Unleashing the Idea Virus*. New York: Free Press, 2000.

Godin, Seth. *Purple Cow: Transform Your Business by Being Remarkable*. New York: Portfolio, 2003.

Kawasaki, Guy. *The Art of the Start: The Time-Tested, Battle-Hardened Guide for Anyone Starting Anything.* New York: Portfolio, 2004.

Kiyosaki, Robert T., and Sharon L. Lechter. *Rich Dad, Poor Dad.* New York: Warner Books, 2000.

Klaus, Peggy. *Brag! The Art of Tooting Your Own Horn Without Blowing It.* New York: Warner Business Books, 2003.

Levinson, Jay Conrad. *Guerilla Marketing: Secrets for Making Big Profits for Your Small Business.* Boston: Houghton Mifflin, 1998.

Levitt, Steven D and Stephen J. Dubner. *Freakonomics: A Rogue Economist Explores the Hidden Side of Everything.* New York: William Morrow, 2005.

Mackay, Harvey. *Dig Your Well Before You're Thirsty: The Only Networking Book You'll Ever Need.* New York: Currency, 1999.

MacKenzie, Gordon. *Orbiting the Giant Hairball: A Fool's Guide to Surviving with Grace.* New York: Viking, 1996.

Montoya, Peter. *The Brand Called You: The Ultimate Brand-Building and Business Development Handbook to Transform Anyone into an Indispensable Personal Brand.* Santa Ana, CA: Peter Montoya, 2003.

Peters, Tom. *The Brand You 50.* New York: Knopf, 1999.

Rein, Irving, Philip Kotler, and Martin Stoller. *High Visibility: The Making and Marketing of Professionals into Celebrities.* Chicago: NTC Business Books, 1997.

Ries, Al, and Laura Ries. *The 22 Immutable Laws of Branding: How to Build a Product or Service into a World-Class Brand.* New York: HarperBusiness, 2002.

Ries, Al, and Laura Ries. *The Origin of Brands: Discover the Natural Laws of Product Innovation and Business Survival.* New York: HarperBusiness, 2004.

Ries, Al, and Jack Trout. *Positioning: The Battle for Your Mind.* New York: McGraw-Hill, 1981.

Rivkin, Steve, and Fraser Sutherland. *The Making of a Name: The Inside Story of the Brands We Buy.* Oxford: Oxford University Press, 2005.

Roffer, Robin Fisher. *Make a Name for Yourself: 8 Steps Every Woman Needs to Create a Personal Brand*. New York: Broadway, 2000.

Sanders, Tim. *The Likeability Factor: How to Boost Your L-Factor and Achieve Your Life's Dreams*. New York: Crown, 2005.

Steinberg, Neil. *Hatless Jack: The President, the Fedora, and the History of American Style*. New York: Plume, 2004.

Trout, Jack, with Steve Rifkin. *The Power of Simplicity: A Management Guide to Cutting Through the Nonsense and Doing Things Right*. New York: McGraw-Hill, 1999.

Trout, Jack, with Steve Rifkin. *Differentiate or Die: Survival in Our Era of Killer Competition*. New York: Wiley, 2002.

Trout, Jack. *Jack Trout on Strategy*. New York: McGraw-Hill, 2004.

Welch, Jack, with Suzy Welch. *Winning*. New York: HarperBusiness, 2005.

White, Ronald C., Jr. *The Eloquent President: A Portrait of Lincoln Through His Words*. New York: Random House, 2005.

Whyte, David. *Crossing the Unknown Sea: Work as a Pilgrimage of Identity*. New York: Riverhead, 2002.

⟨⟨ Index ⟩⟩